SPANISH-SPEAKING HEROES

ROGER W. AXFORD

PENDELL
PUBLISHING
COMPANY

International Standard Book Number: 0-87812-041-6
Library of Congress Catalog Card Number: 72-78441

© 1973 by
Pendell Publishing Company
Midland, Michigan

All Rights Reserved
Published 1973
Printed in the United States of America

NAIDA LARUE AXFORD—MOTHER OF SIX

Who taught us what it means to be

Citizens of the World.

CONTENTS

CONTENTS (Cont'd.)

FOREWORD

The word "hero" brings to mind the idea of heroic action, accomplishment, and success. And, indeed, this is exactly what the author of this little book purports to illustrate; the success of some two dozen Spanish-speaking immigrants or children of immigrants.

America has often been described as the land of unlimited opportunities. Compared with other countries, America offers the newcomer greater opportunities to make a living than most other lands. However, immigrants know only too well the sweat, tears and humiliation they have had to pay in exchange for those "infinite opportunities." The old dream that in America a man can pull himself up by his bootstraps "from rags to riches" is gone forever, not only for the foreign immigrant, but also for the Anglo-Saxon white.

Scholarly books have often described the difficulties encountered by immigrants or members of minority groups in adapting themselves to a new culture and to a new and often adverse social situation. Newspapers and popular magazines, on the other hand, have often emphasized other negative aspects of immigrants: their poverty, lack of employment and schooling and perhaps also their difficulties with the law. However, few publications have emphasized the positive contributions made by immigrants or children of immigrants. This book is one of those few exceptions.

Spanish-Speaking Heroes is a delightful collection of colorful vignettes portraying the life experiences and successes of some Spanish-speaking people in America. These men were immigrants or children of Spanish immigrants who have made a positive contribution to American culture. We find them in all fields and in all walks of life: singers, educators, sport-idols, executives, musicians and labor leaders, to name but a few. They are contributing to the wealth of American culture with the same ingenuity and versatility that characterized the Italians and Germans and the Irish that preceded them.

What makes these *Spanish-Speaking Heroes* worth our admiration and praise is not so much that they have succeeded in making lots of money. Not all of them are making lots of money! And besides, money should not be used as a criterion to measure success. What makes them worth our attention and admiration is their cultural contribution to American society, both in terms of what they have done and in terms of what they are for themselves and for us all. When we read about Roberto Clemente, we are proud of him not because he is the highest paid player in the history of the Pirates, but because he is the best player in the game today. We are proud of Cesar Chavez because he is a uniquely unselfish human being helping America purify itself of injustice and discrimination. We are proud of Pablo Casals not so much because he has played twice in the White House but because he is the world's greatest cellist, because he is a man of conscience, and because he is a stubborn believer in human freedom.

These men, in vastly different fields and in different ways, are making a contribution to American society. We are proud of their successes. Long live the Heroes!

JOSE A. MORENO
Associate Professor Of Sociology
Director of Graduate Studies
University of Pittsburgh

PREFACE

"Blessed are those who cultivate in themselves a love for their neighbors, and who respect before everything the dignity of the human being."

Catherine Breshkovsky

Every society needs its heroes. Much can be told about a community by the kind of people they admire. Unfortunately, only a few real champions are recognized during their lifetime. Regrettably, heroes of another culture are little known or recognized outside their own group. In the United States we know too little about the contribution of Spanish-speaking persons who have bridged two cultures. Few of us know the hardships, the struggles, the sacrifices, and the courage of minority groups. The heroism of parents, who often made possible the success of their children, goes unnoticed. These selected biographies attempt to reveal the strength of character of a few Spanish-speaking victors.

For years I have observed there is insufficient literature available about persons of Spanish background written in English. Working with adult literacy classes, I find few materials with which Spanish-speaking people can identify. I feel success stories are needed to help the "self-image" of Spanish people in an Anglo culture. Herein, an attempt is made for short biographies which can be easily read in five to ten minutes. Included in this edition are persons from Mexico, Puerto Rico, Cuba, Dominican Republic, and Spain. Many others I would like to have included. Interview possibilities and available data impose the limitations. It is

hoped the project may be expanded in the future.

I was inspired by the idea of biographies of Spanish-speaking people by my work with a group of teachers from Venezuela and the Dominican Republic. I served as director of a Latin American project dealing with the comprehensive high school under the Agency for International Development at the University of Wisconsin-Milwaukee in 1963-64. The outgrowth of the project was an invitation from the Ministry of Education of Venezuela to visit their liceos (high schools) and some of their universities. This was followed the next summer by a visit to the Dominican Republic and Puerto Rico. I served as a consultant to the University of Puerto Rico in long-term planning for University Extension.

Comprehensive work with literacy programs in adult education during the last ten years gives me an appreciation of the problems of migrants and Spanish-speaking people in the United States. By knowing first-hand the pain of learning a second language, I can identify with problems of bilingual people.

Since a child, I have been interested in biography. First-hand experience with foreign-born people in the United States has convinced me it is not easy "to make it" in the Anglo culture. Differences in value systems are major hurdles, but language is the greatest barrier, as persons in these biographies confirm. It is my hope that these stories may help both Spanish-speaking and English-speaking children and adults to appreciate the contributions made by people of Spanish-speaking background. Perhaps the reader will see vocational possibilities from these stories.

The face-to-face interviews have been extremely enjoyable, and I wish to express my appreciation to the many librarians who have helped with biographical data where first-hand interviews were prohibitive. Especially, I want to thank Mr. Richard Chamberlain, Reference Librarian, Stabley Library, Indiana University of Pennsylvania, for his interest and help. I would also like to thank the many persons who suggested names to be included, even if space did not permit.

Appreciation is expressed to Mrs. Marilyn Kinter and Miss Debbie Barto for readying the manuscript. Also, many of the faculty of Indiana University of Pennsylvania have given encouragement and suggestions. Special thanks go to Mr. John Sinclair, journalist and teacher, for his helpful ideas.

I am indebted to the late Dr. Fred Eastman, Professor of Biography and Drama, Chicago Theological Seminary and the University of Chicago, for what I have learned about biography. It is he who inspired me to learn how important it is to "crack open" a character and learn his value system.

It is my hope these biographies of Spanish-speaking winners may encourage youth and adults to imitate and surpass the accomplishments of these few chosen. May the account of the struggles of these heroes add richly to our lives; Anglos and Spanish-Americans alike.

ALFRONSO RAMON LOPEZ

BASEBALL MANAGER

We were going past the baseball field in Tampa, Florida. The children saw the name — LOPEZ FIELD. "Who was Lopez?" one of the children asked. I told them gladly!

One of America's great baseball players and managers was Alfronso Ramon Lopez. He was born August 20, 1908, in Ybor City in the Spanish-speaking part of Tampa, Florida. His parents had moved to Florida from Madrid, Spain, and Alfronso's father got a job in a cigar factory. One of Lopez' early memories was of the smell of tobacco, and he decided at an early age to never work in a cigar factory, if he could help it. At age sixteen Al Lopez was playing baseball with the Tampa Smokers. A newspaper account tells that he was offered $150 per month, and he said, "I took it before they changed their mind."

It was in 1959 that Lopez caught for the unforgettable Walter Johnson, one of the great pitchers of baseball history, in an exhibition contest. Johnson said to Lopez at the end of the game, "You're going to make a great catcher some day. Nice game, kid."

Lopez advanced rapidly. In 1925 he played in the Florida State League,

catching for Tampa. Then he was promoted to the Jacksonville team of the Southeastern League in 1927. He was then sold at the end of the season to the Brooklyn Dodgers. He played three games for the 1927 Dodgers, but did not get more than three hits. He was sold the following year to the Atlanta team of the Southern Association. In 1929 he played 143 games and .327 during the season. When Brooklyn took Lopez back in 1930, he had made a place for himself for the rest of his life in the major leagues.

Lopez played for many teams. Although he remained with Brooklyn for six years, having two of his best seasons, he soon found himself sold to the Pittsburgh Pirates. It was in 1934 that Lopez was named to the National League All-Star team. He was with the Pittsburgh

1

Pirates when he again was a member of the All-Star team. He had been traded to Pittsburgh in the middle of the 1940 season after four seasons with the Boston Bees, a part of the National League.

One of the crises of Al Lopez' life was when he was a leader of the Pittsburgh Pirates. An incident happened that embarrassed the management. A Pittsburgh paper conducted an opinion poll among its fans and asked the readers to suggest a successor to Frankie Frisch, who had managed the Pirates. Lopez was the winner by a great majority. But that next year he was traded to Cleveland.

Lopez began his managerial career tutoring Indianapolis. It was a great beginning. Al guided the club to the American Association pennant while the club finished in second place twice, in 1949 and 1950.

Lopez was now in the big time and in the big money. On November 10, 1950, Al was hired by the Cleveland Indians. Lopez was hired for $35,000 a year, hardly to be compared to the salary he received for rolling cigars in Tampa! For six great seasons Lopez managed the Cleveland team. Never did his team win fewer than 88 out of 154 games, an excellent record. They also came home with one American League pennant during that period. But the World Series of 1954 proved a downfall for the Indians when they dropped four straight games to the New York Giants.

So Lopez left the Cleveland Indians in 1956. A month after he quit he was hired by the Chicago White Sox—this time at the enviable salary of $40,000 per year. One of the sports writers told of Lopez in a story for the *New York Times* in 1950 "Lopez is a matchless handler of men, the most important qualification a manager needs. But he has everything else, including a magnetic personality. One extra quality is his adaptability. When he managed Cleveland he had slow-footed power hitters. So he let them slug away, always playing for the big inning. With the White Sox he had speed and no power. So he had them running and the inside baseball was his strength. And he did just as well with the rapier (sword) as with the bludgeon (club)."

Within three years Lopez had the Chicago White Sox catching up with the New York Yankees. Both 1957 and 1958 saw the Sox ending the season in second place. In fact, Al was named the "American League Manager of the Year" in 1957.

The New York Yankees continued to be the greatest challenge for Al Lopez. He was convinced that his club had a chance to win the pennant. He said of the Chicago White Sox, "I love baseball, and I think we have a good chance of winning the pennant." 1958 was a great year for the Lopez team. Preseason polls chose the Yankees as favorites, but they really never got started. Lopez coached his White Sox team to the league championship, which was to be the road to the World Series. The Cleveland Indians and the Chicago White Sox paired off in August of 1959, and his team won a four-game series. They tasted victory by

2

beating Cleveland on September 22 in a 4 to 2 victory.

But Lopez was not always a winner. Lopez continued to give a magnetic spark to the White Sox. He led the Chicago team to the World Series again, but this time the Los Angeles Dodgers proved too much for Al's team. The lively White Sox were beaten in the World Series four games to two. Lopez was known for his graciousness either in victory or defeat, qualities which made him appreciated by the press and the baseball world.

Rumor had it that Lopez would succeed Casey Stengel as the manager of the New York Yankees. But, in 1960, Lopez signed to manage his White Sox team at the "modest" sum of $60,000. After the 1959 World Series, Al was convinced the White Sox were good enough to capture the pennant again. But, Al Lopez hit his pinnacle when in the annual Associated Press poll, this great manager and baseball player was voted "American League Manager of the Year for 1959," for the second time. It must be remembered that the Chicago White Sox had not won a pennant for forty years, and to beat the New York Yankees in the process was sweet victory.

What does a Spanish-American baseball manager do for a hobby? Al likes to play with his son, Alfronso Ramon, Jr., and occasionally takes him hunting or fishing. Although Al likes to hunt and fish, golf is a favorite hobby. Al is never happier or more relaxed than on the golf course. In 1960 Al was shooting between a 78 and an 83.

Alfronso Ramon Lopez was married on October 7, 1939, to Evelyn M. Kearney, and they had one son. Lopez will be remembered as the manager who inspired so many teams to win, and few of his teams finished in less than second place. Like the now famous ad, Al achieved greatness because Al tried harder!

3

CESAR CHAVEZ
LABOR LEADER

"DON'T BUY GRAPES" was the sign being carried by seminary students in Bangor, Maine. When children asked one of the students the meaning of the sign, they were told "You know, the Cesar Chavez strike against the grape growers for better wages and living conditions." Cesar Chavez is known from California to Maine.

Chavez is a short man, described as "growing round around the middle, with a dark walnut complexion, coal-black hair, and restless dark eyes."[1] Chavez heads the powerful United Farm Workers, AFL-CIO, formerly the National Farm Workers Association. And how did this humble grape worker become a national figure? By challenging a $4.08 billion-a-year industry known in California as "agri-business." From California, and largely from the "Central Valley," comes forty-three percent of the fruit and vegetables sold in the United States. This valley depends to a large extent on farm labor, and three counties alone produce an annual crop worth more than one billion dollars of cotton, tomatoes, peanuts, asparagus, apples, plums, grapes, sugar beets, and numerous other fruits. It must be remembered that the farm workers have never been effectively organized.

Unfortunately, they have never had the legislation which safe-guards the rights of industrial workers. There were in 1969, 2,200,000 Mexican-Americans in California, many of whom are farm workers.[2] Eighty-four percent of the Valley farm workers earn less than the federal poverty level of $3,100. For example, in Fresco County, more than eighty percent of the welfare cases come from farm families. And Cesar Chavez became the spokesman for these families.

Chavez knows the hardships of being a migrant worker. Cesar was on the road with the pickers at the age of ten and attended more than three dozen schools. He recalls that he did somehow get through the seventh grade.

Chavez remembers living one winter in a tent. He tells how in 1938 he had to walk to school during the winter in his bare feet because the family was so poor. He helped keep the family from starvation by fishing in a canal and by cutting wild mustard greens. The lack of money made it impossible for his family to leave the camp. Relatives in Arizona finally gave them a few dollars so they could get to Los Angeles. He recalls how his mother and father arose at 5:30 mornings to pick peas in the fields. The boys in the family collected tin foil from cigarette packages and sold it to a Mexican junk dealer. Cesar and his brother got enough money to buy tennis shoes and each a sweatshirt, which had to last them many seasons.

How did Chavez become so well-known and make Delano, California, famous? Located in the San Joaquin Valley, Delano is a small town on Highway 99. It is the grapes that make Delano unique and famous. And Chavez helped to bring the town to the attention of the nation; his cry — the demand of workers for "the right to organize."

Chavez has been described as having what author Fred Ross calls "a sense of quiet power," a sense of mission. He can be both talkative and humorous. He is known to be infinitely patient, and some say that he hates to give orders. Even though he is extremely busy with his work, he will stop and listen to the most simple problems of any striker. Chavez once had a carload of food delivered in front of his house at 2 a.m. Instead of just giving directions to the driver as to the location of the camp warehouse,

Cesar got dressed and took the man out to the camp and helped him unload the truck.

It was to give dignity to the farm worker that the strike began. Chavez thinks not only of this generation but of coming generations. He said to the Senate Subcommittee on Migratory Labor, "Some people say, write off this generation of parents and hope my son gets out of farm work. Well, I'm not ready to be written off as a loss, and farm work could be a decent job for my son, with a union."

Chavez fought so that the farm worker can have a living wage. He said that the average farm worker in Delano has seven children, rents a house for $55 monthly, makes payments on furniture, a car, and often to a finance company. Before the strike, the Mexican farm worker worked eight months of the year at $1.10 per hour, and most often his wife worked beside him. Summers and weekends the children were in the fields, too. Chavez says, "This average farm worker buys food at the same stores at the same prices as the rancher does. And he's not making it. So now, these average workers are strikers; they've been willing to lose their cars, furniture, to live on beans and more beans, to work 'on the line' seventy hours a week for the right to a living wage."

What kind of a childhood would produce this leader of the grape workers? Cesar Estrada Chavez was born in Yuma, Arizona, one of five children. His father, for a time, had a small farm near the

Colorado River but went broke trying to make a living. It was when Cesar was ten that the family started following the crops. He remembers that they moved from one labor camp to another. This was Depression time, and workers were numerous, and jobs were few. Chavez recalls that those days when his family first went to California were rough, hungry days. Chavez tells how his family was often exploited, made to work for little or nothing. One contractor near Fresno had his family working seven weeks, promising to pay when the winery paid the contractor. He remembers vividly, "We were broke, absolutely broke, with nothing at all to eat, so the contractor finally gave us twenty dollars and said we'd get a big check later when the winery paid him . . . we haven't seen him to this day."

The family was poor and desperate. He tells how green his father was and how many times they were fooled. They learned little tricks like living under bridges. And they finally learned where the crops were, and when the farmers needed workers. It was in 1939 when the Chavez family was working San Jose. The CIO union was organizing the dried-fruit workers, and Cesar's father and uncle joined the union. He remembers seeing picket signs and hearing union talk at his home. Cesar remembers clearly his father and uncle picketing during a strike, picketing at night. It made a deep impression on him. He also remembers they lost the strike. Cesar was nineteen when he joined the National Agricultural Workers Union. He served in the United States Navy in 1944-45 and then, returned to migrant farm work.

Chavez is best known for his organizing the blanket boycott of all California grapes, begun in 1968. More than two hundred union workers spread across the United States and Canada to tell the story. They organized support in thirty cities, getting backing from city officials in Boston, New York, and Detroit. For example, St. Louis officials directed their municipal purchasing agents not to buy California grapes. Even stores in Maine refused to buy grapes. In August, 1968 a *Wall Street Journal* report told that 20 percent of the national market had disappeared as a result of the boycott. But Chavez sees his labor organization as more than traditional unionism. His 50,000 workers[3] have "a cause," "a movement," and their leader wants to see his union involved in politics, in voter registration, and in more than just contract negotiation. Chavez is fearful of the industrial union model, where the grower might become the organizer, just checking off union dues. He wants to have a cross between being a movement and being a union. He is fearful of centralized power in the hands of only a few. Chavez wants the union membership to maintain basic control.

Chavez met his wife Helen in Delano, and she has been described as a "remarkably stalwart woman." The family is Roman Catholic and now has eight children. Humble and dedicated to lifting his fellow Mexican-Americans out of almost economic slavery, Chavez can best be described in the words of the late Robert F. Kennedy who said, "He is one

of the heroic figures of our time." He is a
modern Moses to many of the agricultural
workers of the United States, and his
influence is still growing.

---

1 John Gregory Dunne, Delano, The Story of the California Grape Strike, Farrar, Straus, and Giroux, N.Y., 1967, p. 57.

2 New York Times Encyclopediac Almanac, 1972, p. 237.

3 Letter to author June 22, 1972 from Blase A. Bonpane, Director of Publications, United Farm Workers Organizing Committee, AFL-CIO.

GREG MORENO

HOTEL MANAGER
Hyatt Corporation
San Jose, California

Greg Moreno was born in Tcalitlan, Mexico, in the state of Jalisco on June 10, 1944. His father, Silvestre, worked hard and went to school to learn to become a lawyer and now has a plantation in the State of Jalisco raising coconuts, bananas, and lemons.

As a boy, Greg loved sports. Specifically, Greg liked to play football, baseball, and basketball. But he remembers that even as a boy he "always wanted to exercise some sort of power." Unlike many boys in Mexico, he enjoyed his school classes. But most of all, he liked world history, mathematics, and geography. He remembers that even as a boy he always wanted to travel. Especially, he wanted to go to Europe some day. But, instead, he feels that good fortune helped him end up in the United States of America.

Greg's education included elementary and high school in Mexico, where he received his high school diploma. He earned another high school diploma when he came to the United States. Following high school, he attended two years of college at San Jose State College in California. He decided he would like to study business and majored in business administration.

One of the things he remembers most clearly is attending adult education courses in San Jose. He took two courses at a time, English and history. He remembers most vividly two teachers, a Mrs. S. Holmes, and a Mrs. Stone. Both ladies taught him English for foreign-born students. "English was fun," Greg tells, because of the special interest shown in him by the teachers, and the materials used in the classes. Greg is very proud that his is now a citizen of the United States. He took out citizenship in June, 1970. Greg related how he was drafted and wanted to tell about his war experiences. He spoke of how he was wounded in Viet Nam. Greg was shot in the chest and leg and was hospitalized but returned to the front lines after many days in the hospital. He has great hopes that peace may come to the world. Greg says he often wonders if people really want peace, because there is so much fighting in the world.

The real break came for Greg Moreno when the Vice-President of the Hyatt Corporation, Mr. Albert J. Kelly, befriended him. Mr. Kelly gave Greg encouragement and hope for advancement. Moreno says of him, "I think Mr. Kelly thinks of me like one of his own family." He saw to it that Greg had the same chance for opportunities and promotions as any other person in the hotel business, and hired him at his San Jose hotel. He encouraged him to work hard and to advance in the hotel industry. Greg has worked in almost every position available in the hotel business. For example, in the six years Greg has worked, he has been a bus boy, waiter, bellhop, captain, and auditor.

Today, Greg is the Assistant Manager of one of America's most beautiful hotels, the Regency Hyatt House in Atlanta, Georgia. The hotel is thirty-two stories high, and Greg supervises the more than 1,000 rooms. While working in San Jose, he learned the many jobs needed to be done to have a hotel serve its guests effectively. Greg was not transferred to the Regency Hyatt in Atlanta until he returned from the army to San Jose. Then Mr. Kelly gave him the opportunity to work in management at the unique Atlanta hotel. Greg went to Atlanta as a "management trainee" and was then promoted to the Assistant Manager.

He likes the hotel business and especially likes working with people. He knows most of the workers by name. "Most of all," Greg says, "I like a chance to serve the public in the best possible way."

One of the persons who helped Greg when he was trying to get an education was Dr. Raymond McCall, the San Jose California Director of Adult Education. "Dr. McCall encouraged me to take courses such as accounting, speech, business English, and typing. The school provided me with a scholarship which took care of books, tuition, and materials. Most of the persons were from foreign countries," Greg relates. He remembers vividly that the school had persons attending of all ages, both young and old. Greg says that he has found little prejudice and adds, "Being Spanish makes no difference, but it depends upon the individual himself, and what he wants to do with his life. I think a person can open his own doors of opportunity provided he is capable and has a real desire to succeed."

"One of the most important things one needs to learn is to communicate effectively and to make sure one is properly understood," says Greg. He feels that honesty and integrity are most important, and being trustworthy is most valued. Although Greg enjoys working with people, he reminded me, "Of course, we work with all kinds of people," How true that is in the hotel business, and Greg was called away a number of times as a "trouble shooter" during the interview. A number of people wanted his help and advice. When I interviewed him in Atlanta, he had just had the maids make a linen count to see how many pieces of linen had been taken by guests and needed to be replaced. So, hotels have problems of things "disappearing" Greg said.

10

Greg said that he considers his greatest accomplishment, thus far in life, is getting an education. He is also very proud of being offered and holding his position as a hotel executive. But, Greg has not quit learning. He is continuing to learn by taking classes which the hotel provides for the employees. Greg takes courses in personnel administration, hotel management, food services, and in human relations. He encourages young men to go into the hotel business and to work their way up. He feels that the vocational schools can offer opportunities for training, if young people are interested.

Greg has the dream of someday having his own hotel. He told me he finds very little time for recreation, but he does enjoy golf, and plays golf now and then. Football is one of his favorite sports. He is also very fond of baseball. The team he likes best is the Atlanta Braves, and he sees them play quite often in Atlanta.

Greg was asked what are his hopes for the Spanish-American people? He responded, "I hope that there may be better relations developed between the Spanish-speaking people and all those in the United States." Because he is willing to learn, work hard, and be of service to others, Greg may have only begun his climb to fame as a hotel manager. "Buena Suerte" Greg! Good Luck!

TRINIDAD LOPEZ, III

SINGER

Known for his Latin folk rock, Trinidad Lopez is a singer popular throughout the United States and the world. Rated as one of the ten top singers in a popular music survey, his "surf sound" has been heard on records and in night clubs throughout the land. "Sinner Man" and "If I Had a Hammer" have made him famous, and young people try to imitate him in style and tone. One writer has described his music as "hypnotic," and the combination of his voice and his amplified guitar send teen-agers into shouts and screams of joy. Trini can make the most stiff and stuffy adult succumb to tapping his foot and singing along with Lopez.

Born of Mexican parents, Trini, as he is popularly called, started life on May 15, 1937. He was born in Dallas, Texas, and likes to put "3rd" after his name, since he is the third to use the name Trinidad. His father worked hard and became the superintendent of grounds at Southern Methodist University. Trini knew the hardships of slum living, for he was brought up in a one room house in the Spanish-American side of Dallas. Trini learned English after he entered high school. He spoke only Spanish until that time. He was one of six children, with four sisters, and a brother who played the saxophone and liked to sing. The boys often sang together, and Jesse, his brother, started a singing career under the direction of Trini. At an early age the Lopez family enjoyed music and the Lopez children were encouraged by their parents to make something of themselves.

Many people learn by imitation. And so did Lopez. He watched his father sing and play, and we are told Trini, then, taught himself to sing and play. He would play and listen to Frank Sinatra and Ray Charles' records and try to learn from them. It was a bright day for Lopez when his father bought him a guitar and encouraged him to learn and play. As a young boy he organized his own combo and soon was playing some of the best restaurants in Dallas. He and his musical group were hired at big night clubs in the Southwest region. He was pleased to get a booking at Los Angeles at the Ye Little Club. What started out as a two week engagement lasted for a year. Lopez made

a hit in the Los Angeles area, for he was then booked for extended runs at Ciro's and P.J.'s, well-known nightspots. Then, the musical director of one of the recording companies heard him sing, taped his act, and asked Frank Sinatra to come and hear the tape. Frank Sinatra was then the principal owner of Reprise Records, and this was the beginning of the big time for Trini.

It was in 1963 that Lopez signed an exclusive contract with the recording company. Not long after that, Trini caught the interest of one of the most capable managers in show business, George "Bullets" Durgom. Durgom heard Lopez sing and play and immediately signed him to a long-term contract.

Don Costa, the musical director of the Reprise Records, turned out to be a real friend to Lopez. One of the first records that he made was like the tape he had made at P.J's. That album was called TRINI LOPEZ AT P.J.'S and became a golden record. He sold more than 4,500,000, when only one song was released on a single record, by title "If I Had a Hammer." Some of the songs in the album are "This Land is Your Land," "La Bamba," "Granada," "Gotta Travel On," "Down By the Riverside," and "When the Saints Go Marching In."

A tour of Europe took Lopez to many countries. In 1963 and 1964 he sang to standing room only crowds. He sang in such places as the Olympia Music Hall in Paris. By the middle of 1964 Lopez was commanding $5,000 for a single performance. With his own eleven man orchestra, Trini made his musical debut in New York and was a smash at Basin Street East. One of the newspapers in New York praised his performance by saying, "His phrasing is impeccable and his approach to a tune is completely original." Critics gave him a friendly word which helped his career. One said of his singing, "All he shares with the rock groups is his rock rhythm." On top of this he puts his Spanish words, old favorites, blues, new hits, and a nice stage personality. In a period of five years he cut twelve albums.

He found it fun to record with regular accompanists Dave Shriver as a bass guitarist and with Gene Riggo playing the drums. Some of the big engagements were at the Palmer House in Chicago, the Riviera in Las Vegas, the Off Broadway Club in San Francisco, and Reno's own Harrah's. He played concerts in many foreign countries including Japan, the Philippines, Africa and Australia. The Reprise Records cut most of his albums including; MORE OF TRINI AT P.J.'S, TRINI LOPEZ ON THE MOVE, THE LATIN ALBUM, THE FOLK ALBUM, and many others. He has appeared on many TV shows and in a film comedy with Sinatra and Dean Martin . . . *Marriage on the Rocks.*

Trini Lopez was voted the "Man of the Year" award by Dallas, Texas, in 1967. Trini is what is called, in the music world, "a natural." Singing seems to be second nature to him, and his whole being becomes a part of song. The Spanish people gain emotional power from this voice that expresses strong emotion. Many of his records are already becoming collector's items.

PABLO CASALS

CELLIST—CONDUCTOR

"A man of conscience" is the way Pablo Casals is described by a biographer. For one of the world's greatest cellists and musical conductors has lived in exile voluntarily to protest the rule of Franco in his beloved Spain. Casals lived first in France and then in Puerto Rico, where he now makes his home. How vividly I remember seeing this dynamic musician lead the Casals Festival Orchestra in the Music Hall of the University of Puerto Rico. It was the summer of 1965, and eighty musicians were gathered from all over the world to play under the direction of this great man. First violinist and concert master, Alexander Schneider, seemed to almost dance to Casals' baton. And Casals was 89 years old! I remember his expression of appreciation when backstage I brought him a large glass of water after a rehearsal, while I was working for the University of Puerto Rico.[1] His youthful wife is constantly by his side with a large satchel, including a towel and his medicine. (A more gracious lady you will never meet!) Early morning rehearsals of the Festival Casals draw music lovers and students who have affection for this great maestro. He now conducts

only seated, but he has the apparent strength of a young bull.

Born with the full name of Pau (Catalan for Pablo) Carlos Salvador Defillo de Casals, he was surrounded with music from birth. Pablo was born in Vendrell, a town about forty miles from Barcelona, Spain, on December 29, 1876. His father was a strong liberal, and all his life Pablo has felt that a musician should not remain aloof from politics. Pablo's father was a church organist, so that at an early age he was receiving music lessons. Casals says that from childhood music was for him a natural element, "an activity as natural as breathing." As soon as he could reach the pedals he was playing the church organ. And he sang in perfect pitch, so that at the age of seven he was singing, transposing music, and even composing music. The story is that

1 I would attend the morning rehearsals held in the University of Puerto Rico Auditorium for the Festival Casals, before going to the office where I served as Consultant to the University of Puerto Rico Extension Division in 1965.

the first cello Pablo had was an invented instrument owned by some traveling minstrels. Pablo's first cello was made out of a gourd for a sounding board and is still a family treasure.

His father taught him violin, piano, and gave him lessons on the organ. At eleven years of age Pablo went to study with Jose' Garcia at the Municipal School of Music in Barcelona. Like many parents, the mother and father did not agree on what Pablo should become. His mother wanted him to become a great musician. His father wanted Pablo to become a carpenter's apprentice. But who won? His mother took him to Barcelona and placed him with relatives. As a boy he was serious and sensitive. But he had periods of depression brought on by disagreements between his parents. Pablo had his light and happy times, however, for he earned a living for himself and some of his family by playing for dances at the Cafe Tost.

Then, Pablo Casals went to Madrid where he lived for three years. These were important years. He was under the patronage of the Count de Morphy and Queen Cristina. He got a 250 peseta scholarship from the Queen. He studied composition and learned chamber music which proved very important in his career. He became quite close to the Royal family. But, we are told he did not let this influence his political judgments. From Madrid, Pablo's mother took him to Brussels, Belgium. Here, his mother felt he could develop his talent in cello. He stayed in Belgium a short time, and the family went to Paris. In Paris, young Pablo earned only four francs a day as a cellist at the Folies Marigny, a hall of music. But his earnings helped keep the family together. Family savings were small, and the family finally returned to Catalonia.

Casals taught at the Municipal School of Music in Barcelona. He also played cello at the Barcelona Opera, and he gave several concerts. At the age of twenty-two, he was earning enough money to give the family financial help. So, he returned to Paris alone. November 12, 1899, was an important day for Pablo. He studied with Charles Lamoureaux and made his Paris appearance as a virtuoso, an accomplished musician. Twelve long years he studied the Bach music. By then he had mastered the suites, the music for cello. Audiences learned to love his interpretation on the cello, and he raised the level of musical taste through his playing and conducting.

Making Paris the center of his activity, Pablo played all over Europe. He toured the United States more than a dozen times playing concerts. In 1914 he helped to found a school of music known as the Paris Normal School of Music. He became well-acquainted with leading musical personalities of the time such as composer Maurice Ravel and violinist Fritz Kreisler. Then, after the first world war, Casals decided to give his energies to his beloved land of Spain. He founded the Pau Casals Orchestra in Barcelona in 1920 and put a good deal of his money into the project. We know that he supported the Orchestra to the extent of about $320,000. He worked for the Orchestra giving money and his talent until it was self-supporting. Casals loves to conduct. Anyone who has seen him in action knows that he lives most energetically when he conducts. It is the human teamwork that seems to inspire him. He says that the *teamwork* demanded of musicians in an orchestra is what he calls the "greatest of all instruments."

Casals likes to compose and enjoys playing his cello. As early as 1904 he played in the White House for Theodore Roosevelt, and many years later played for the late President John F. Kennedy. In 1958 he gave a cello recital at the United Nations. It was in 1964 following the visit with President Kennedy, that he told Norman Cousins, Editor of the *Saturday Review* "I was very happy in my heart." He had spent more than an hour privately with Kennedy, discussing the problems of world peace in an atomic age.

Casals feels that the working man should have a chance to enjoy good music. He wanted to reach the working classes, and so he founded the Catalan Workingmen's Concert Association. For only six pesetas a year the member could attend some of the great performances. They could hear the Pau Casals Orchestra. And Casals encouraged the organizing of local musical groups. He loved and lived for music. One of the favorite pieces Pablo likes to conduct is Beethoven's Symphony No. 9. And he had opportunities to conduct some of the greatest orchestras. For example, he was guest conductor for the London Symphony, led the New York Symphony Orchestra, and had the honor of leading the Vienna Philharmonic Orchestra.

Casals is a lover of human dignity as well as music. He feels that the artist must be involved in politics, and he protested the cruelties of the Russian regime in 1917 by refusing to play in that country. He also protested the Hitler regime, and the facist government of the 1930's. Then, when Franco took over Casals' beloved Spain in 1939, Pablo went into voluntary exile that will not end, he says, until the people choose their own government. He performed benefit concerts for victims of Franco Spain.

Following the German occupation, Casals stopped all public appearances and remained in silence at Prades, a town in southern France. He committed himself to helping Spanish exiles held in neighboring prison camps. He turned down attractive offers in the United States, because he did not want to leave his friends who also had taken a strong stand against dictatorships. Casals is one of the heroes of freedom!

Casals has, since 1962, annually brought the Festival Casals to the Carnegie Hall in New York City. But, if you want the thrill of a lifetime, take a week in June and travel to Rio Piedras and hear and see the great Maestro at the University of Puerto Rico. Your spirit will be lifted, and you will have seen one of the world's great cellists, a world famous conductor, and a fighter for freedom. And, as a bonus, if you are lucky, you may get to meet his gracious young wife who herself is an accomplished cellist, a queen of the music world. And for her, as for many, the king of music is Pablo Casals!

JOSEPH MONSERRAT
PUERTO RICAN EDUCATION CHIEF

Known as the first Spanish-American to head the Board of Education for the City of New York is the energetic Joseph Monserrat. For many years Monserrat headed the Migration Division, Department of Labor, of the Commonwealth of Puerto Rico and helped thousands of persons coming from the beautiful island to live in New York City. Monserrat surrounded himself with many strong people such as Matilda de Silva of the University of Puerto Rico School of Social Work. His life long friend and educator, Leonard Covello, first Italian to be principal of a New York high school, he used as an advisor-consultant. The *New York Times* speaks of Mr. Monserrat as "a hard man to keep up with," for he is a hard worker and demands more of himself than he does of his busy staff. His secretary, Mrs. Anna Figueros, finds him a tireless man, even working at the office on weekends. She won't answer her phone on the weekend, for she knows it is Monserrat working. She says, "He never stops working. He works day and night. And if you let him, he wants everybody else to work as hard as he does. Nobody can work like him," according to the *New York Times*.

Monserrat has the human touch and the milk of human kindness, for he has known hardship first-hand. He was born on September 17, 1921, in Puerto Rico but came to New York when he was three years old. For seven years, he lived in a foster home. He rejoined his father when his father remarried. Joseph then moved into East Harlem in New York City where he lived with his father and stepmother.

He attended the New York Public Schools. Following high school, he joined the United States Air Force. He returned to enroll at Columbia University and pursue his interest in social work. He attended the New School for Social Research which has some of the most progressive and socially minded professors of any university in America. The school brought many refugees from Europe to teach, and Joseph Monserrat came under the influence of these great

19

teachers. He dedicated himself to helping the Puerto Rican migrants coming from the sunny homeland and finding themselves in the often cruel city.

Monserrat has many accomplishments of which he can be proud. For example, he has been a member of such groups as the New York Moreland Commission on Welfare, The New York State Advisory Committee to the United States Civil Rights Commission, The New York City Council on Manpower Utilization, and the Mayor's Committee on Exploitation of Workers. It is his purpose on these committees to help the poor and to make more and better jobs available to Spanish-speaking Americans. Because education proved to be a real help to him and opened many doors, he believes strongly in the importance of education. It is for that reason he has given thousands and thousands of hours to the education programs in New York. His belief in education is the reason he agreed to be the president of the New York City Board of Education, probably the largest school operation of its kind in the United States.

Mr. Monserrat lives with his wife Josephine and daughter Laura. We are told that he was the life of the party when his daughter was married. He enjoyed telling his friends that he had gained a younger brother in his son-in-law. He is extremely fond of his young daughter, and the story is that on Father's Day, daughter Laura sends her father a card for brothers. Friends say Monserrat treats his daughter as though she were a younger sister. I remember

meeting Monserrat in his office in the Puerto Rican Division of Migration of the Department of Labor, and his friendly welcome sets the stage for all his workers. His humane touch carries over from his family life to his office, and his devotion to human betterment.

What does Monserrat think of his responsibility as a member of the New York Board of Education? He says: "Few contemporary issues are as pertinent, far-reaching, and yet confused as is the issue of education in a democratic society. In our city and nation today, this issue is surrounded with fear, anger, hate and even hopelessness." And with more than a million Puerto Ricans estimated to be living in New York, Monserrat knows what he is talking about. He wants to replace fear with trust, anger with concern, hate with understanding, and "to spur hope and pride in our education system."

Joseph Monserrat is one of the persons who has seen to it that Puerto Rican migrants flown to this country are not exploited. Through his leadership in the Commonwealth Department of Labor, strong contracts have been demanded from the growers before they can use the workers who are flown over for the harvest from Puerto Rico. A unique aspect is that each group of workers must have a teacher of English accompany the pickers. This has meant that Puerto Rican migrants have had a chance to learn reading, writing, and simple arithmetic evenings after a day of picking fruit, vegetables, or packing. Learning English has helped many a worker get a job in New York. Monserrat has demanded that laborers not be exploited, and that their rights be respected. He has also helped to bring Adult Basic Education to the Puerto Ricans in the City of New York.

Monserrat worked in the settlement houses after his schooling in social work. He was one of the very early street workers to deal with gangs as a member of the New York City Youth Board.

Many people wonder how Mr. Monserrat can accomplish so many things. He keeps a busy schedule. But, he says, "When you're busy you make time. You begin to choose priorities more carefully." One of his high priorities is education. Another is helping the poor. As the "tireless Board Chief" Joseph Monserrat is making a name for himself as a public servant and as a leader of the Puerto Rican people. Both New York and the nation will do well to keep an eye on this leader of men, the "Puerto Rican Education Chief."

RICO CARTY

BASEBALL'S "TORMENTOR OF PITCHERS"

Described as a "Tormentor of Pitchers," Rico Carty is one of the Atlanta Braves' proud players. And Atlanta is proud of No. 25, sometimes called "one-tenth of a ton of bone and rippling muscle."

Rico Carty's full name is Ricardo Adolfo Cababo Carty. He was born on September 1, 1940, on a sugar cane plantation near the seaport of San Pedro de Marcoris in the Dominican Republic. Rico Carty managed to escape the cruelty of Trujillo and has been playing baseball in the United States for ten years. At first, Rico did not want to stay in the United States. He was homesick and wanted very much to return to his father, mother, and his fifteen brothers and sisters.

Rico, as he is known to the fans, says he was mean. He used to fight as a boxer. He says, "I was so mean I wouldn't even talk to people. I was just a complete mean fellow . . . . and still when I came to baseball, I was mean; I want to trample everybody. I'm glad I'm not this way anymore." In fact, Rico is beloved by the kids. He enjoys autographing baseballs for children and is now warm and outgoing. Rico has one of the hottest baseball bats in the league. We know that now he loves the fans, and the fans love him back. What were Rico's greatest hurdles? Two things were difficult for Rico—the English language and a fight with tuberculosis in 1968.

Many adults can sympathize with Rico, for he struggled with the English language. His basic language is Spanish. One sports writer asked Rico, "Your English is good. How did you improve it?" Rico told him he had a chance to improve his English when he was in the hospital. He said, "When I was sick in the hospital with tuberculosis in 1968 I went back to school again and studied English. They learned me grammar. One teacher told me that's what I need. She really helped me." So Rico turned a bad thing, sickness, into a learning situation.

Rico is known for his smile. He says it was in Davenport, Iowa, where the fans first started cheering him. He says, "If I make an error, you see me smile. That's the way I am. That's my natural way of being. But here in the big leagues you find lots of people think you're making fun of the game if you smile. But, that's my way of being to keep myself from getting mad." Rico's smile has won him thousands of friends. For example, when he was in the hospital he got mail from 8,000 Atlanta fans alone. He was amazed and delighted to receive get-well mail from 15,000 persons during the six months he was in the Lantana Hospital. Mail came even from other countries, which made baseball's hero very happy. He even got a letter from Greece. He was very surprised, he said, and it made him so pleased and happy to think that people thought about him and prayed for him and wanted him to come back and play baseball. He thinks his friends helped him get well. They no doubt did.

Many people wonder why Rico Carty catches the ball with one hand. Rico tells that he learned to catch the ball with one hand because in the spring of 1961 he broke a finger on his right hand. They made him play everyday anyway, because the regular catcher hurt his back. They made him catch with one hand because of the broken finger, and he just kept on playing with one hand ever since. He says he got so good at catching with one hand that now he never catches with two hands. And the fans love it!

Rico's success can be observed in his strength, his good batting eye, and his rhythm. He says that the good eye and rhythm come natural. "No one can show you how to do it," comments Rico. "They can show a player how to stand, how to hold the bat, but they just can't show you how to hit." He thinks there is no substitute for experience. He thinks it is mighty important to know the strike zone. Timing is of greatest importance. He feels that his timing is good, and attributed his good hitting record to watching the ball carefully and getting his timing right.

One of the questions young people like to ask Rico is what makes a good hitter? His answer is that it has to come naturally. One of the managers he is especially fond of is Luman Harris, whom he describes as out of this world. He says Harris is different from any manager he has ever seen. Rico hit .300, .310, and .326 in the first three years with the Braves. In May of 1970 he was the National League "Player of the Month." And much of this success he gives to Luman Harris. "He'll resolve your problem any minute. And I mean he is just great," says Rico of Harris. He feels he had problems with every manager, except Harris. He confides this is the only manager who really understood him, and he really enjoys playing for Harris.

Rico Carty is affectionately called "Big Boy." Many people want to know where he got the nickname. He says that Joe Torre was the first person to call him "Big Boy", and he thinks it is because he used to "play around" a lot. He remembers a time in Milwaukee when he would be signing autographs and when there would be signs in left field welcoming him. Torre would say, "Boy, you are something else." And from then on they would call him "Big Boy." When he went to Atlanta, the nickname went also. "So when I came here, I used to say, the 'Big Boy' is here now, so don't worry. The 'Big Boy' is here." And the nickname seemed to stick, and Rico seems to like it.

Rico has some strong feelings about human relations and specifically race relations. He feels strongly about prejudice between the races and talks about it in interviews with sports writers. He comes from a country where he says, "You can do what you want. Everybody likes you, as long as you are decent. Nobody's going to like a nasty person. I find that I'm free to do what I want, and I love people, and people love me." He feels that we can overcome prejudice, but he says to overcome the problem it will be years and years. He feels the young people can solve the problems, and he has faith that they can and will.

Rico especially likes kids. Rico says that the manager got after him when he would give away so many baseballs. But Rico replies, "I like people, especially kids. I used to throw them baseballs even in the minor leagues." One of the Milwaukee Braves coaches used to get after Rico when he would throw baseballs to the kids in the stands. But he told the coach, "Well, why don't you just go ahead and take it out of my check?" That's the kind of a fellow Rico is. But he has a friend in Jim Nash who said that Rico brings fans to games this way. Nash thought, "If Rico gives six balls, a dozen or more balls a game, just think how many people are going to come see Rico play because maybe their kid will get one."

Rico Carty is a very religious man. He says he is thankful to God for his health being better. He gives credit for his success to his religious faith. "I haven't been hurt, and I'm grateful for that to the Almighty God, and I have to thank him," volunteers Rico. He says, "Without Him, nothing can be done."

Rico wants most to hit over .300. He says after that he is satisfied. He wants next to win the batting championship someday. And if he keeps his smile, his health, his eye on the ball, and hits the ball like he has been, he may be that batting champion. He was the all-star catcher in the Northwest League in 1962. As a National League rookie in 1964, Carty was runner-up to Roberto Clemente for the batting title and second in the "Rookie for the Year" balloting to Richie Allen. Keep an eye on "Big Boy" Rico Carty — tormentor of pitchers!

Born in a small town in the northern part of New Mexico called Chamisal, meaning "sagebrush," Jose' P. Lopez says the village is made up of persons with Spanish blood and some Indian blood. His father and many generations before him lived in this village. His father did not receive a formal education, but Jose' describes his dad as a "very intelligent man." He did learn to read but, of course, in Spanish. It was his father's dream to become a businessman, and for thirty-five years he owned sawmills. He learned to mechanize his mills and finally ended up with two fine ones.

Jose' feels that the hardships encountered by his family are typical of many Spanish-American families living in New Mexico. The lack of proper medical attention stands out in Jose's memory.

His father wanted, particularly, to see his ten children obtain an education. The national mission of the Presbyterian Church played an important part in Jose' getting an education. His father was able to send all the children to the mission school in Sante Fe.

Jose' went to the Menaul School, a high school sponsored by the church.

Jose' was the 1000th graduate, he recalls. Teachers came from all over the country, from New York to Oklahoma, offering a rich variety of experiences.

Jose' remembers that when he first went to school, he was fearful; and because of the unfamiliar surroundings he returned home. He would not stay there because he yearned for the village he had known. But the next day after he returned home, his parents took him back to the school, driving the entire sixty miles. "My parents really valued education," Jose' recalls.

Like many children, Jose' had his dreams. He always wanted to be a medical doctor. The way doctors could help people appealed to this young boy, for he could see the pain which the physician could relieve. But he feels his education was inadequate. When teachers of English would talk about the best

known literature, Jose' knew little of the American writers. "Often I did not know what the English teachers were talking about. Of course we studied Anglo literature. I realized I had to acquaint myself with the Anglo literature if I was going to succeed in this culture. When I went from the high school to the university, then I realized how many obstacles I had to overcome in English." Jose' graduated from high school in 1952, and his grades were good enough to obtain admission to the university. He found the university catalog confusing and difficult to read. After two months in the university he was drafted, and was in the army for two years. But one of the crises of his life was when he returned to school. He had taken German, chemistry, physics, and was headed toward premedical training. Even though he had been deferred, he learned that he had never been notified of a deferment. On his return to the university, he learned that he had been given 18 hours of F—or failure. He thought he had withdrawn correctly but found he had been counted as a dropout. It took two years for him to convince the university of his military call and official withdrawal. He returned to the university as a part-time student.

At Allison James High School, Jose' had met and courted Eulogia Herrera. Upon his return from the army, he asked Eulogia to marry him. She accepted. Being a stenographer, his wife went to work to help Jose' through school. Describing himself as a "struggling student," his wife obtained a $35 a week job. In 1956 Eulogia got a job with the Sandia Corporation. "My wife worked side-by-side with me," relates Jose'. Sometimes studying part-time, sometimes full-time, Jose' finally graduated in 1965 from the University of New Mexico.

Jose's first job out of college was with the Paul Revere Insurance Company. He had worked part-time with a freight line. He worked his way up from a dock-worker to a job in customer-relations. Jose' followed his insurance experience with a position with the Employment Security Commission of New Mexico. He took a cut from his insurance pay, "but this is what I wanted to do," says Jose'. He enjoyed the year there but felt limited by bureaucracy.

Jose' learned that the New Mexico Labor and Industrial Department received a grant through the Equal Opportunities Commission to conduct a program for job training. Jose' was selected to work with both employers and employees. He was hired as an educational officer for the Fair Employment Practices Commission, and for nearly a year he worked for the FEPC.

Then the leaders of the American GI Forum and LULAC, the co-sponsors of Jobs for Progress, approached Jose' and asked him to consider working for them. "I wanted to lead; I did not just want to follow," he says. George Hernandez called and asked Jose' to take a leadership position. In July, 1968 Jose' met with the board and was offered a position with Jobs for Progress.

When asked who were persons who most influenced his life, Jose' remembered a Dr. Donaldson of his high school as a major influence and friend. Jose' describes himself as "a terror" in high school. His teachers felt Jose' was energetic and creative and should use his talents for positive purposes. Dr. Donaldson seemed to say to Jose' as he describes it, "Please, Jose', let me channel your energies some other direction." Dr. Donaldson wanted Jose' to be a preacher. He and Dr. Donaldson had a number of heart-to-heart talks about this. He asked Jose' to join the gospel-team, and Jose' did. Jose' was worried that he showed in his personality too much anger and not enough compassion. He questioned how good a minister he would be. But Dr. Donaldson continued to encourage Jose' in his education.

Jose' volunteered that he was aware of a problem of his "self-concept." He did not feel he was as good as his Anglo friends. He thinks there is a good reason for his feelings. Jose' recalled a vivid incident. He remembers when his father was in the lumber business. Jose' would go with his father who, unfortunately, would have to wait while others were taken care of. "Often the white people would be taken care of first, when my father stood next in line. I felt bitterness about this. I never said anything about it, but I felt it inside. So, I grew up thinking I had to be second or third all the time," Jose' related. "I told myself, 'when I get physically strong I am going to retaliate'."

Jose' remembers walking into a social security office in 1962 and inquiring for his father about retirement benefits. I could see my Spanish people from the northern part of New Mexico being interviewed by non-Spanish-speaking people. The English-speaking employee could not understand this humble Spanish-speaking man. It made Jose' angry. I felt they were being treated like foreigners in their own country. Jose' inquired there and went to his senator's office to see if conditions could be changed. Change came. "Today there are Spanish-speaking interviewers. It took two years, but it was worth the fight," confided Jose'.

Jose' feels one of his greatest accomplishments was getting an education. There were moments when there was little time for study. In the process, he even got an ulcer. He wondered if he could really make it. College was his biggest goal and his greatest hurdle. Now, he feels the obtaining of a degree can be over-emphasized. But his education opened doors.

His next greatest accomplishment, he feels, is joining Jobs for Progress, a program funded by the Department of Labor and the Department of Health, Education, and Welfare of the United States Government. In his work, he has done a special study of the "self-concept" of the Spanish-speaking people. He would like to pursue this in greater depth.

In answer to the question "If you could have dinner with any person you wished, living or dead, except Jesus Christ, who would you choose?" Jose' answered, "I think my first choice would be the late President John Kennedy. One other person I might add would be Martin Luther King."

Jose' feels that his Spanish-American background gives him an appreciation of his culture. "The family ties, the sentiment of becoming a responsible father, what it means to be a responsible husband, what society has done to provide me with a good wife, and what I can pass on to my children, all are valuable," says Jose'. "The ability to know and to use two languages is an advantage. To use Spanish to learn English is an advantage. For example, the word, capricious, is a Spanish concept. "I find many words in English similar to those in Spanish," relates Jose'.

Jose' loved to read as a boy. Fortunately, Jose's father was, what he called, "educationally oriented" even though not formally educated. As a boy, not being able to speak much English was a real handicap for Jose', and language he feels was a major hurdle for him. He now speaks and writes both English and Spanish fluently. "It really helps in my work," he says.

Jose's hope for the Southwest is to develop a community representative of all the people. "I hope I can help my people enjoy the better things in life. I want for them to be able to be educated, to be businessmen, to be all of these, and still retain their culture. That is my hope." Jose' is active in adult education organizations both in the Southwest and on the national level to help his Spanish-speaking people attain their and his goals.

Jose' walked out of the hotel room to the National Adult Education meetings with a certain dignity and pride that was evidenced in his step. He had shared with the author his lonely experiences as a boy, as a Spanish-American struggling to get an education, and to get and maintain a job. Now he had told his story, and he said he hoped to inspire other young Spanish-American people not to give up, but to seek education, to take their studies seriously, and to be proud of their Spanish culture.

Jose' feels there are many opportunities to serve human beings through the government agencies, if Spanish-speaking people will take the initiative and train for the jobs. Jose' has proved it through his leadership in Jobs for Progress. He can be imitated.

ROBERTO WALKER CLEMENTE

"PUERTO RICAN SUPERSTAR!"

Brown-eyed, black-haired Roberto Walker Clemente was born on August 18, 1934, in the little Puerto Rican town of Carolina but now resides in Rio Piedras, Puerto Rico. He lives not far from the beautiful campus of the University of Puerto Rico, when the baseball season is not on.

Clemente has been described as the "most complete ball player in the game today." He was drafted by the Pittsburgh Pirates from Montreal in November of 1954. And the Pirates are mighty proud of him. This year was the 16th season as a Pirate. He has the enviable record of having a lifetime major league batting average of .314. And Roberto Clemente is the *first* Latin American to ever win the National League batting championship. And he has done it *four* times, three times under the Pirate Manager Danny Murtaugh. His .314 lifetime batting average is the highest among active major league players. An outstanding record!

Standing five feet, eleven inches tall, this one hundred eighty pound slugger is the envy of many a baseball player and fan. Before 1968 Clemente was the only big leaguer to hit .300 or better every year since 1960. He is among the Top Ten in the Pittsburgh club history in twelve different offensive departments. For those who watch Clemente, he is known as a daring and exciting runner, and he is often responsible for making the game winning hit or game saving play. He is described by one sports writer as "a Puerto Rican Superstar" and Clemente is known for his outstanding pride and he excels in most everything he does. Roberto Clemente has been a Gold Glove Winner nine times. In 1966 he had the distinction of being chosen as the National League's MOST VALUABLE PLAYER.

Clemente has exploded the theory that a baseball player's peak years are between about 23 and 29. Another idea Clemente has proved false is that a player in baseball should retire in his mid-thirties. His best years started at age 26,

and he is still going strong after 16 years, just with the Pittsburgh Pirates.

In 1966 Clemente set a record in his career for homers with 29. A baseball player is often judged best by an outstanding player from another team. Dave Briston, one time manager of the Cincinnatti Reds has described Roberto as "the best player in the game today. I'd have to take him over Aaron, Mays and all the rest."

Roberto Clemente is now known to be the highest salaried player in Pittsburgh Pirate history. This is because of his all around ability as a baseball player. Clemente has twice hit three home runs in one game, on May 15, 1967, and on August 13, 1969. He is one of two hitters in history to hit two homers over right centerfield at now vacant Forbes Field where the wall marker is 436 feet. One sports writer admits Forbes Field is one of the most difficult in the big leagues for any batter, and adds, "If he played in a smaller one, there's no telling how many home runs he'd hit."

It is well-known that Clemente never gives up or lets up when playing ball. Has he had some hard times? In 1969 Roberto injured his left shoulder when diving for a ball. He got off to a bad start and unfortunately only hit .242 in his first 27 games. But in the next one hundred and eleven games he hit .373, a remarkable improvement. Then he hurt his back on September 5, 1969 in Chicago. He was 9 for 44 from September 6 to September 20. Then he had eleven hits in the last five games hitting an average .515. That fell just three points below winning the batting title! Even with shoulder injuries the past two seasons Clemente has been able to throw with considerable accuracy, and with great strength. He has one of the most feared and respected arms in baseball. So, he has learned to overcome handicaps, and has come out a champion.

In 1967 Clemente set a Major League record by leading the National League outfield assists for the fifth time. Clemente says that when he feels strong he can hit any pitching, and his record proves it. One of Roberto's dreams is to manage a baseball club someday. He often plays baseball for the San Juan Senators when he is in Puerto Rico, where he spends most of his winters. In 1970-71 he managed the Senators. He is held in affection by his friends in Puerto Rico for they have asked him to run for Mayor of San Juan, but he has refused to do so while he is still playing baseball.

In 1971 Pittsburgh's Roberto Clemente was the leading hitter in the World Series. He ended the regular season needing just 118 hits for a lifetime total of 3,000. This is a record achieved by only 10 men in baseball history.

In 1965 Roberto built a lovely fifteen room home for his gracious wife Vera Christina Zabala whom he married on November 14, 1964. The Clementes' have three sons — Roberto Jr., Luis, and Enrique.

Former Milwaukee Braves Felipe Alou says of Clemente, "You take liberties with other guys you never take with him. He's always thrown out five or six of our guys at home plate." He is known as rifle-armed Roberto. He hits the ball like a bullet, and every pitcher fears him when he comes to bat. He won the Dapper Dan Award both in 1961 and in 1966. He is truly a superstar, and many a Spanish-speaking youth can look with pride to this National League Batting Champion.

On December 31, 1972, Roberto Clemente died as the plane carrying him and four others crashed into the stormy waters of the Atlantic Ocean off the coast of his native Puerto Rico. Clemente, heading the Puerto Rican earthquake relief effort, was taking supplies to the survivors of the Managua, Nicaraguan earthquake. Waiving all rules and regulations, Roberto Clemente has been installed in the Baseball Hall of Fame, in honor of his baseball achievements on the diamond and his personal achievements as a member of the human race.

MARGARITA HUANTES

SAN ANTONIO'S FIGHTER AGAINST ILLITERACY

Adult educator Margarita Huantes is a fighter for the right of every adult to learn to read. Mrs. Huantes is working daily in behalf of the 128,000 illiterates over eighteen years of age in San Antonio. She never gives up. She started the San Antonio Literacy Council, Inc., in 1962. Her first small office was in the basement of a downtown Presbyterian Church which offered space. The office is only a stones throw from the Alamo. Mrs. Huantes worked nights and weekends recruiting volunteers for her literacy program, insisting every adult has the right to know how to read and write.

The Literacy Council in San Antonio became a dues-paying organization under Margarita Huantes' leadership. She got free services from a friend in public relations. She convinced the mayor to declare a "Literacy Week" and got free radio and TV time. Soon there were six literacy centers, and following the Literacy Week campaign eight more centers opened.

Recognition of Mrs. Huantes' efforts for illiterates was made concrete in the 1965 United Fund campaign in San Antonio when $10,000 was given the Council. Immediately, Mrs. Huantes hired

more part-time teachers needed so badly. These helped the volunteer teachers. Eventually her teaching staff expanded to 100 teachers. Often up to 2,000 persons not able to read or write were learning in the centers.

Why does Mrs. Huantes think this work so important? San Antonio has the highest percentage of illiterates in the State of Texas, one of her flyers tells. Ten and one-half percent of the San Antonio population are functional illiterates, reading and writing below the fourth grade level. Mrs. Huantes wants these adults to vote, to learn skills so they can get jobs, to learn to read instructions on medical bottles, and to take better care of their children, helping them with their school work.

Mrs. Huantes says, "We cannot afford to ignore our problems in San Antonio! One out of every six adults in our city is illiterate." OPERATION AWARE, sponsored by her council and the Texas Literacy Council, is recruiting "sponsors" saying that $10 can provide education for one student for one year. Individual membership is invited at $1.00 for a year. One year, when the students learned of the possibility of classes closing, they raised $800 just among themselves. They said that they are the ones benefiting from the reading and writing instruction. The adult students then organized a fiesta and barbecue, and raised $1,000 which they gladly gave the Literacy Council.

Have there been some discouraging times? There surely have, confides Mrs. Huantes. In January, 1967 the funds for the adult education program ran out, and it appeared the program would have to be dropped. Like heroes of learning, many of the paid teachers just continued on as volunteers. The San Antonio United Fund had hoped to give $10,000 but did not reach its goal and could donate only $5,000. But then a wonderful thing happened. In August of 1967 the Bexar County Education Agency expanded its adult education program into the county school districts. This included San Antonio, and the Literacy Council was saved. It got a share of the funds. Soon materials and books written at the elementary adult level were made available. Adult basic education teachers were recruited and trained by the school system. Then some of the foundations learned of the work of Mrs. Huantes and the Literacy Council and made some grants to the reading and writing program. The program expanded its budget to $15,000 in 1969 and to $20,000 in 1970. Much of the success of the program is due to the fact that Mrs. Huantes is always working for the Council and is a hater of illiteracy.

Where did Margarita Huantes get her drive and interest in helping fight poverty? Some persons say her interest in education is due to the fact that she had to quit college for a time to help her three sisters get an education. But she never gave up her goal of a college education. She attended summer courses at the University of Texas. After getting her bachelors degree, she went on to school to study social work at the Western Reserve University in Cleveland, Ohio. There she got her master's degree.

After her training as a social worker, Mrs. Huantes returned to San Antonio, Texas. She had always had a firm determination to work against poverty and fight illiteracy.

One day Mrs. Huantes attended a conference with a group of social workers. The conference was in 1960 and was held at Baylor University in Waco, Texas. Here she saw a colorful exhibit of the work of the Baylor Literacy Council. "Why not a San Antonio Literacy Council?" she asked herself. And her mind was made up. She went to work with all her heart and energy. And the San Antonio Literacy Council was born in the Inman Christian Center, where

36

persons from eighteen to seventy are learning to master skills. Many learn enough so they can pass the high school equivalency test, and some earn diplomas.

Mrs. Huantes is now a member of the Executive Committee of the Adult Education Association of the U.S.A. — a national organization representing persons from libraries, migrant councils, university extension, public school adult education, and many volunteer organizations such as the YMCA's and YWCA's. But, the thing that means most to Mrs. Huantes is that meeting when she was the Director of the Inman Christian Center, now the Mexican Christian Institute — when she called that meeting to try to organize a local literacy council. She was overwhelmed when all thirty-six members attending the meeting agreed to help with the council, and all agreed to teach.

Is Mrs. Huantes satisfied? No! Not until the San Antonio Literacy Council reaches at least ten percent of the illiterates — 18,000. Her annual report says that there are 23,000,000 (million) functional illiterates in the United States, and that 180,000 live in the greater San Antonio area. This past year 496 volunteers helped in the reading and writing program, and more than 2,500 persons were helped. In one year the Literacy Council operated 42 centers with a total of seventy-two classes. But Mrs. Huantes never gives up, and she says, "We have the challenge which has not been met." She is still training teachers, recruiting volunteers, and raising money for the right of every adult to be a self-respecting citizen with the ability to read, write, and vote intelligently. Mrs. Huantes always will be known as "San Antonio's Fighter Against Illiteracy!"

(Thanks is acknowledged to Doris Wright, editor of The Light in San Antonio, Texas for biographical material which appeared in American Education, November, 1970.)

DR. MARI—LUCI JARAMILLO
EDUCATOR,
PROMOTING HUMAN UNDERSTANDING!

Mari-Luci Jaramillo was born in Las Vegas, a small town in northern New Mexico. Her father was a Mexican national, who had come to the American dream during the Pancho Villa days. Her mother had come from a farming community near Las Vegas.

The family was poor. Although the father was a talented musician and leather craftsman, money was difficult to obtain in the 1930's. The family, consisting of Mari-Luci, a younger brother and an older sister, lacked experiences that material wealth can bring through things such as trips and books. But they were blessed with a mother who gave them love and encouraged them to "do their best always."

Mari-Luci started school without knowing English. She recalls seeing children waving their arms when the teacher would speak. Wanting to join in, she would raise her hand but after teacher called her name three or four times and there was silence and then children giggling, she realized she needed to know more of what was going on. She quickly learned that a student raised her hand only if she knew the answer the teacher wanted.

By the end of the first year, she had become an excellent student by the school's standard. She was quiet, polite, and attentive to school work. From then, she was always honored as one of the best students in all her classes.

Although reprimanded occasionally for speaking Spanish, she refused to join many of her peers and "forget" her native language.

The positive reinforcement which she received at home, to be proud of her Spanish heritage, made her a true biculturate at a young age. She learned two norms of behavior and was equally at home with Spanish-speaking friends as well as with English-speaking friends.

Her elementary and secondary schooling continued without interruption. Her ingenious mother found ways of supplying new cardboard soles

for her shoes every night. She also found that a small can of enamel painted her white summer shoes into stylish black ones for winter. The remaking of hand-me-down clothes from friends and neighbors kept her in style. A dress could always be lengthened with a ruffle.

Having no electricity or central heating was not a problem. Her mother lit a kerosene lamp and bundled her daughter with blankets where she sat at 5:00 in the morning to "cram" a little. This was the time Mari felt she learned more.

She continued receiving excellent school grades and was named valedictorian of her graduating class. She received all five awards given at commencement. In those days there were no scholarships.

She had worked after school and on Saturdays cleaning a lady's home, as well as working in her father's shoe repair shop for extra money. She continued this work following her high school graduation. Between her and her father, they were able to save the money for tuition at New Mexico Highlands University her freshman year. She never bought books; she borrowed her friends' books.

At the university, she became involved in all the activities that didn't cost money. She continued getting excellent grades, but she still wore clothes made from pretty "feed" sacks her mother would save pennies to buy.

She had grown tall but was still as skinny as a rail. She remembers pressure from close friends to "fatten up a bit."

Her appetite was poor, but she had more energy than anyone. She read everything she could get her hands on, be it in English or Spanish. She loved to dance, and a favorite pastime was practicing new dance steps with her brother or close friends.

At the end of her freshman year, she married and left the university to live in a small rural area in northern New Mexico. She quickly became a part of the community and helped in school activities and surrounded herself with the neighborhood children.

After two years of rural life, and now with a small son, she returned to Las Vegas. She wanted to return to the university but had no money. Working at small jobs and saving from the family's small income, she returned to Highlands.

Then she started on a cycle of education and work. She worked at a factory for a semester and saved enough money to attend the university the following semester. Then she would repeat this again.

During this time she had another son and a daughter. Her mother babysat so Mari-Luci could work and study.

The semester before graduation was crucial in her education. The factory had closed, and she did not have the money to return to school.

A teacher, Miss Nell Doherty, who had taken a personal interest in Mari-Luci's education, realized what was happening. She offered her $200.00 with the understanding that if Mari could, she would repay. If she couldn't, when the opportunity arose she was to help some other student in any way she could.

She was able to repay Miss Doherty both ways. The following semester she was named to "Who's Who in American Universities." With her first pay check, she paid her debt. She has been able to repay the other half of her debt by helping several students with the little "extra" needed, be it encouragement or financial aid.

Mari-Luci taught school in rural New Mexico for several years before she returned to her home town to teach. She taught in the elementary school, later becoming a remedial reading teacher, and finally the Language Arts Consultant for the West Las Vegas School System. She constantly tried to find ways to improve teaching of minority group students.

During these years, she earned a Masters Degree with "Honors," at Highlands University, attending school at night and during the summers. Upon receiving her Masters, she became a visiting instructor at Highlands during the summers. She also worked in teacher preparation during the school year.

After eight years of teaching in Las Vegas, the family moved to Albuquerque. She taught three months in a barrio school before being invited to join the faculty at the University of New Mexico.

Upon joining the University of New Mexico, she found herself deeply involved in work with Latin American Education. She was made assistant director of the Latin American projects. For several years she traveled frequently to the majority of the countries in Central and South America. She enjoyed the work immensely because she was actively involved in promoting human understanding.

With her children almost grown, she decided to continue her education. She enrolled at the University of New Mexico as a doctoral student. Since she was her own sole support, she continued working, with most of her studying done during the night and on weekends. Her sister became her typist for all her class work, as well as for her dissertation.

In 1970 she was awarded a Doctor of Philosophy degree in Education. She was made assistant professor in the College of Education. She continued to travel, adding Asia and Europe to the countries she had visited.

Today, she is actively engaged in a Civil Rights Project, still pursuing her lifelong interest of getting a better education for everyone. She contends that the education of one person is the work of many people.

MATTY ALOU

DOMINICAN CENTER FIELDER

The Atlanta Braves had just won after the game had been tied 7-7. In the 10th inning Matty Alou's St. Louis Cardinals were beaten by one run. But it was Matty who had hit that ball, scoring two players, bringing the Cards from behind to tie the game. Matty catches a fly like a bird perches on a tree. I made up my mind to interview him. With his smiling voice, he consented. We met at the Atlanta, Georgia, Marriott Motel where the team was staying.

I met Matty as he was heading from his room to the lobby. A big smile and soft voice told me this must be the Dominican Republic's gift to baseball. He graciously invited me in and the questions began. My limited Spanish helped some. Sometimes we spoke in Spanish, sometimes in English.

HOW DID YOU
GET INTO BASEBALL?

"Every day we play baseball at home. The whole family, my sisters too. My sister, Maria, is a very good ball player. She's fast. We are four brothers and two sisters. We all play baseball in the backyard, since we were little kids."

WHAT DID YOUR FATHER DO?

"He was a carpenter and a black-smith. We made horseshoes. I helped him. We lived on a small farm and raised goats, lots of them, four horses, and chickens. I didn't know then they paid baseball players," he laughed.

WERE YOU DISCOVERED BY
A BASEBALL SCOUT?

"Yes, I didn't know there were such things as scouts. But, we had a good friend of the family, Horatio Martinez. He saw us play baseball. He was a scout for the New York Giants and got my brothers interested in playing professional baseball. I started with the Michigan City Giants in 1957."

43.

WHAT DO YOU THINK OF AS YOUR FUNNIEST EXPERIENCE?

"Well, I had taken my wife to the theater in Santo Domingo. I got up at the movie and went home without her. Then I remembered I had left her at the theater. By the time I got back she had already gone home."

HOW MANY YEARS OF SCHOOL DID YOU HAVE, MATTY?

"I went to school through the 10th grade in Santo Domingo, in the Dominican Republic. Yes, I learned a little English in school, but mostly I just went to school. I picked up most of my English here in the United States."

WHO DO YOU CONSIDER TO BE ONE OF YOUR HEROES?

"I think it would be Gil Hodges, manager for the Mets. We used to sneak into the park and watch the Brooklyn Dodgers. Also, I used to like to watch them when they came to Santo Domingo for their spring practice. I think he is great."

HOW DO YOU FEEL ABOUT RACE RELATIONS IN THE UNITED STATES? IS THERE PREJUDICE?

"I think it is easier for a white guy to get a job than a black man or Latin American. But right now, it is getting better. I think there is more publicity for the white players. Maybe, that is because there are more white people watch baseball. (He laughed) They pay to see the game."

DO YOU HAVE A SPECIAL HOPE FOR THE DOMINICAN REPUBLIC? FOR THE SPANISH PEOPLE?

"I hope the people of the United States will treat us like others. We are closer to the United States than France or England. It might be because of our color; they don't treat us the same."

IS THERE ANY ONE PERSON WHO HELPED YOU MOST IN PLAYING BASEBALL?

"I think that would be Harry Walker, Manager for the Houston Astros. He helped me a great deal with my hitting. I learned a lot from him."

DO YOU HAVE A SPECIAL HOPE FOR YOUR SON, MATTY, JUNIOR?

"I just want to have a clean life until I die. I want to see my boy grow up to be nice people. I hope he is a good boy for my country and for the whole world. I don't know if it is possible to have peace in the world. I hope so. I think the important thing is raising good people from the father in the family.

WHAT IS THE HARDEST THING FOR A BASEBALL PLAYER?

"The trips are too tiring (Matty was packing when I came to his room). We have too long a season. We play 162 games. That is too much. It should be about 100 games for the season. The fans would have a chance to see better baseball. I always try to keep myself in good shape. I like to run hard before the game.

I work hard in spring training. I like very much to play center field. I like it best because I have been playing it all my life."

DO YOU HAVE ANY SPECIAL ADVICE FOR YOUNG PEOPLE?

"I like kids from this country, especially kids age around eight to twelve. They love baseball. I think sports are good for kids. I think it is important to believe in God. When you are going bad that can really help. My family really helped us. We had to be home early at night, and my mother was tough with us. I don't think we ought to give kids too much freedom. They will follow anyone sometimes. This is a nice country. It is too bad to see so many young people going wrong; it is because of the family. I think people should give more attention to their kids. The best education can be given in your own house."

TELL ME SOMETHING ABOUT YOUR FAMILY, MATTY. WHERE DID YOU MEET YOUR WIFE?

"I met my wife, Theresa, as a neighbor. I knew Theresa since we were kids. She lived next door, and we saw each other often. My son is Mateo, Junior, seven years old, and my daughter is Theresa age five. They are in Santo Domingo, living."

YOUR BROTHER JUAN STARTED OUT TO BE A MEDIC, WHAT HAPPENED TO HIM?

"My mother wanted Juan to be a doctor, but he turned out to be an engineer. The other three of us are playing baseball."

WHAT ADVICE DO YOU HAVE FOR YOUNG MEN WHO WANT TO BE A BASEBALL PLAYER?

"Baseball is like any other business, you have to be smart. To try to be a good hitter, you have to work. You can be a natural hitter, but you have to work hard to get better. I'd say, ask questions of other hitters. Know yourself, that is what is important. Know your main problem and try to work on that problem. To have to wait for the ball, I think that is my biggest problem. I get excited and get in front of the ball. I guess that is a problem for everybody learning to bat."

HAVE YOU EVER HAD ANY ACCIDENTS THAT HURT YOU IN BASEBALL?

"I have good health. But I did have an operation on my leg when I played for the New York Giants in 1963. Well, we travel back to St. Louis pretty soon, so I have to pack."

A more gracious and smiling gentleman you will hardly find. He picked up a clean, new baseball and said, "What's your boy's name?" Then he autographed that white ball with red string "To Scott Axford, Sincerely, Matty Alou." Matty had made one more American boy happy.

JOSEPH M. MONTOYA

SENATOR FROM NEW MEXICO

Joseph M. Montoya climbed to the position of a United States Senator from a humble background. Born in the obscure county of Sandoval in New Mexico, he spent his childhood among the cactus and sand of that western state. He was born on September 24, 1915. He completed his high school education in New Mexico and then went on to college in Denver, Colorado. Following his graduation from Regis College in Denver, he was determined he would become a lawyer. All his energy he put into going to a law school. With the money he had saved and with a burning desire to be admitted to the bar, Joseph M. Montoya headed for Washington, D.C. There he enrolled in the Georgetown University Law School and worked his way through law school. In 1938 Montoya was graduated from the Georgetown University Law School and soon was admitted to the bar. Even at an early age he was engaged in a number of business enterprises, meeting many influential leaders both in New Mexico and throughout the West. Even while he was in college he engaged in politics and made many friends which proved to be most helpful in years ahead.

At the age of twenty-one, while still in college, Montoya was elected to the New Mexico House of Representatives. That was in 1936. It has been said that nothing succeeds like success, and Joseph M. Montoya, Democrat from New Mexico, proves the truth of the saying. He was re-elected to the New Mexico House of Representatives in 1938 and was named the majority floor leader. Then, he was elected to be a member of the State Senate in 1940. Because of his leadership, he was named the majority whip of the Senate. He held the distinction of being elected the youngest State Senator at the time. In 1944 he was re-elected to the State Senate and subsequently was named chairman of the powerful Senate Judiciary Committee. All the time, however, Montoya had his eye on the United States Senate in Washington, D.C. But, the state of New Mexico needed his talents and recognized his leadership.

Montoya then went on to the position of Lieutenant Governor, elected in

1946 and re-elected to that post by the people of New Mexico in 1956. During the period when he was not serving the State as Lieutenant Governor, he was returned to the State Senate and served from 1952 through 1956.

Joseph M. Montoya, now known as the Democrat from Santa Fe, New Mexico, was elected to the 85th Congress of the United States on April 9, 1957, to fill the unexpired term caused by the death of Antonio M. Fernandez. Montoya was now to become a regular member of Congress, and Washington, D.C. was to be his other home. He was re-elected to serve in the 86th, 87th, and 88th Congress. Then, he decided it was time to run for the Senate.

After a hard fought political battle, Montoya was asked to fill the unexpired term of Senator Dennis Chavez. He was subsequently elected to the full term ending in January 3, 1971. He is now a member of a number of powerful committees in the Senate. He serves on the Senate Committee on Appropriations, a key committee. He also serves on the Public Works Committee and the Select Committee on Small Business.

Because of his knowledge of Spanish and his interest in the Spanish-speaking people, he has been invited to international conferences. He served as a delegate to the Mexico-United States Interparliamentary Conference from 1961 through 1965. Montoya served as an official United States observer to the Latin American Parliamentary Conference, Lima, Peru, in 1965. He has been most helpful in problems dealing with United States foreign policy and the countries of Latin America.

Joseph M. Montoya, attorney, statesman, inter-American representative, friend of the small businessman, has given an example to young Spanish-American youth of the Southwest who want to enter politics. He progressed from being the youngest member of the New Mexico House of Representatives to the honor of becoming a member of the United States Senate—one of 100 Senators in the United States.

Montoya married Della Romero. They have three children named Joseph II, Patrick, and Lynda. When they are not in Washington, D.C., they all make their home in Santa Fe, New Mexico.

DENNIS CHAVEZ

SENATOR
FOR
FAIR EMPLOYMENT PRACTICES

Leadership is part of the history of the descendants of Dennis Chavez, the late Senator from New Mexico. One of Dennis Chavez' relatives was a governor of what is now New Mexico, back when it was part of Mexico. It was during the period when Mexico had won independence from Spain in 1821.

The future United States Senator was one of eight children. He was born April 8, 1888, at Los Chavez, Valencia County, in what was then, Mexican territory. He was born into the household of a poor Spanish family, David and Paz (Chanchez) Chavez in Albuquerque. He was baptized Dionisio, but when he went to school he became Dennis. At the age of thirteen, Dennis dropped out of school. He was in the eighth grade when he went to work. He was only a boy when he got a job driving a grocery wagon. He described his job as being a valet to a horse at six o'clock in the morning. He remembers he received two dollars and seventy-five cents a week.

How did Dennis Chavez get to the United States Senate? One writer says that Dennis was deep into politics before he could even vote. Even as a boy he took

to studying Jefferson. He admired Thomas Jefferson and became a Democrat partly through the influence of his writings. Also he rapidly became aware that the schools and the teachers in the Democratic districts of his state were better than the Republican districts.

Dennis got invaluable experience as a Spanish interpreter for Senator A. A. Jones. It was Senator Jones who gave Chavez a help in the 1916 campaign by giving him a clerkship in the United States Senate. Here he began to make political friends. While in Washington, D.C., Chavez took advantage of the opportunity for more schooling. He attended Georgetown University while a clerk in the Senate. Fortunately, he passed a special examination at Georgetown, since he had dropped out of school, and had never gone to high school. But he learned rapidly and in 1920 received his law

49

degree. Dennis was now thirty-two and a lawyer. He was determined to return to his native state of New Mexico and to make a name for himself. He set up law practice.

Then Dennis Chavez started his political career in earnest. He ran for the New Mexico House of Representatives and was elected. In 1930 he determined he would campaign for the United States Congress. After a hard fight he won and went to Washington, D.C. He had defeated a banker and became New Mexico's only Representative in this State with so small a population. Chavez continued reading about his hero, Thomas Jefferson, and spent evenings in the public library studying.

When Herbert Hoover became president of the United States, Chavez was a minority member of the U.S. House of Representatives. But in 1932 he won re-election on the Franklin Delano Roosevelt political ticket. However, he had his political ups and downs. In 1934 he had a hard fought battle with Bronson F. Cutting for the seat in the U.S. Senate. Chavez lost, but contested the election. But it did no good. Then suddenly, Senator Cutting was killed in an airplane accident, and Governor Tingley appointed Chavez to take the Senate seat. His appointment was approved in November 1936, although five senators vigorously opposed his appointment.

Chavez served on many committees such as Education and Labor, Post Offices and Roads, and Irrigation and Reclamation. He took a special interest in the Committee on Territories and Insular Affairs and developed a special feeling for Puerto Rico. He was known as a "New Dealer" and supported the Roosevelt Administration program. Especially, he supported the housing legislation. In 1937 he led and fought for the Navajo Indians who protested the cut in grazing stock proposed by the then Indian Commissioner. He demanded an investigation of the Government plan to make the Indian tribes self-sustaining. The Chavez-McAdoo bill of 1938 supported a Federal radio which would compete with Nazi broadcasts in the Latin American countries. Unfortunately, he urged the United States to recognize Franco Spain. But he fought for extension of trade with Latin American countries, with some success. When Franklin Roosevelt was elected for a third term, Chavez rode to victory for a six year term as Senator in 1940. He won 103,194 votes, while his Republican opponent received only 81,257.

Chavez' interest in Puerto Rico and the problems of the Island brought him the affectionate name of "Puerto Rico's Senator." In 1942 Chavez got Senate approval to investigate the social and economic conditions of Puerto Rico. Five thousand dollars was appropriated by the Senate for investigation. He and his committee chairman, Rafael Bosch, investigated the food shortage and the Island's unemployment. In only two weeks of study by the committee, it reported the deplorable conditions were caused by overpopulation and war conditions. Some of the great progress that the island of Puerto Rico has made may be traced to this initial interest by the Senate in the problems of the Island. In 1943 Chavez and Taft got the Senate to pass a bill continuing Federal works projects both in the Virgin Islands and in Puerto Rico. It was Chavez who proposed native born Major General Pedro del Valle of the Marines for the Governorship of the island of Puerto Rico.

But fair employment practices were high on the priority list for Senator Chavez! In 1943 Chavez was a co-sponsor in the Senate of the Equal Rights Amendment. It was he who said, "Wherever the common law, unmodified by statute, exists, there injustice to women exists." The Senator from New Mexico received national fame when he fought a long fight for the Fair Employment Practice Committee. He insisted in 1944 that the appropriation of five hundred thousand dollars was not enough but would help better our relations with Spanish-American countries. He felt fair employment practices money should be beneficial in showing our sincerity to Latin Americans. As head of the Education and Labor Subcommittee of F.E.P.C., Chavez insisted that twenty-three other times Congress had outlawed racial and religious discrimination when passing laws for public works. It was his bill which was approved in May, 1945, despite the opposition·of five Southern Democrats and a Republican. But Chavez won-$250,000 for a Fair Employment Practices Commission, only half the amount recommended by the Bureau of the Budget. Many states followed this example and established state fair employment practices groups.

This quiet, soft-spoken Senator fought for the rights of minorities, and especially the Spanish-American.

JOSE' TEODORO MOSCOSO MORA RODRIGUEZ

"SELF-HELP" AMBASSADOR! —
CHIEF OF ALLIANCE FOR PROGRESS

"So that's where Theodoro Moscoso, 'Evangelist for Progress' lives," I said as I looked over the beautiful city of Ponce, Puerto Rico, from the hill of the International Hotel. The ten year head of the Alliance for Progress, a ten year multi-million dollar cooperative effort in economic development with Latin America, was headed by the imaginative and capable Moscoso. He had been chosen by President John F. Kennedy, who had the idea in 1961, and chose Moscoso to head the enterprise.

Moscoso was born on November 26, 1910, in Barcelona, Spain. His father, Teodoro Moscoso Rodriguez, was a pharmacist who moved to Puerto Rico; and young Teodoro helped his father and learned the business. Both of Teodoro's parents were American citizens. Young Moscoso graduated from Ponce High School and was elected class president as well as serving as captain of the debating team. He expected to join his father in his drug business and attended the Philadelphia College of Pharmacy and Science. He was editor of the school paper called *The Scope*. Entering the University of Michigan, he majored in chemistry and graduated in 1932 with the bachelor of science degree.

From 1932 to 1939 Moscoso learned management as general manager of his father's drug firm in Ponce. Very early Theodoro became interested in housing, and the problems of housing for low-income groups. In 1938 he became Ponce's leading member of the municipal housing authority. At night he studied housing problems and techniques of building. In 1941 he was made executive director of Ponce's housing authority.

Governor of the Island, Rexford G. Tugwell, saw the talents of Moscoso and in 1942 appointed him housing administrator for all the island of Puerto Rico. What a grand opportunity to experiment with public housing, for Puerto Rico is overcrowded! Soon changes were taking place. Five huge housing projects were built for slum-dwellers. Operation Bootstrap, known as Fomento, was one of the brain-children of Moscoso. Greater

industrialization for the Island was the objective, and Moscoso wrote much of the legislation. He was the first president of Puerto Rico's Industrial Development Company, the government corporation organized to bring industry to the Island. It worked.

Moscoso was part of the brain trust for the billiant Governor Luis Munoz Marin. Offering considerable tax exemptions (from 10 to 17 years), plus a good labor supply, industry could be attracted to the Island. More than one thousand industries are now on the Island of Puerto Rico. The economy was formerly tied to sugar, coffee, and tobacco. The employment rate rose, and industrial schools were opened throughout the Island. Per capita income rose in twenty years from less than $200 to over $600 per year. People lived longer. Formerly people averaged forty-six years of life, but seventy years became the average for life. In twenty years, the industries produced up to $1,000,000,000 in annual payrolls. Tourism was encouraged. Luxury hotels were called "Moscoso's Folly" but laughter turned to envy when $50,000,000 per year was added to Puerto Rico's income.

Then came the Alliance for Progress, known in Latin American as La Alianza Para el Progresso. The Alliance was established by President John F. Kennedy who wisely appointed Moscoso co-ordinator. Kennedy had in March, 1961, appointed Moscoso United States Ambassador to Venezuela. Moscoso was the first Puerto Rican to serve in such a post. He won over many of the leftist students in Caracas who burned his automobile not long after he arrived. He said, "I was a boy once myself and had the same urges." The assistant administrator for Latin America in the Agency for International Devlopment was the post given Moscoso with confirmation by the Senate on February 5, 1962. The Alliance for Progress started when twenty American Countries (not including Cuba) signed the charter in Punta del Este, Uruguay. The purpose was to give financial and technical aid to build up democratic institutions in Latin American countries. "Self-help" was a special emphasis. The design was to deal with housing, agrarian reform, education, health, and tax reform. The United States pledged $20 billion to Latin American countries to be matched in many cases by self-help programs.

Moscoso welded the administrative machinery to make the Alliance work. He worked with the Inter-American Bank, Food for Peace, Peace Corps, and the Organization of American States. Kennedy appointed Moscoso to the Inter-American Economic and Social Council of the Organization of American States — a post which had been vacant for years.

The Alliance for Progress grew under the leadership of Moscoso. By March, 1963 he reported the following: 140,000 dwelling units built, 8,200 new classrooms, 900 new hospitals and health centers, 4,000,000 textbooks produced and distributed, 160,000 farm credit loans, 1,500 drinking wells and water systems, and 15,000,000 people received food from surpluses of the United States. Land reform had started in twelve countries. Tax reform was started in eleven countries. Progress was slow, but Moscoso was an evangelist for progress. Moscoso believed that "nothing succeeds like an idea when its time has come."

This leader knew that the Alliance could not succeed with only economic growth. He knew and stated that we are dealing with human aspirations and emotions. He said the Alliance was not just economic charts, bricks and machinery. But, the Alliance gave hope, asked countries to present long-term development plans, and initiated self-help programs. Often Moscoso was disappointed by the gap between the Alliance's goals and actual results, but he never gave up. He fought like a stag hound for his programs.

Teodoro Moscoso is married to Gloria Sanchez Vilella. They have two children, a son, Jose Teodoro, and a daughter who entered the Peace Corps — Margarita. Moscoso's friends affectionately call him "Teddy." He is known to speak with a slight Spanish accent. In Puerto Rico Moscoso's political affiliation is with the popular Democratic party. He is Democrat and a Roman Catholic. His hobbies include painting, listening to music, and reading. He is an able public speaker, and works sometimes sixteen hours per day.

Moscoso feels that he has a real mission in life. For some time he had on his office wall a sign which says, "Please Be Brief — We Are 25 Years Late!" Many honors have come to this leader of the Alliance for Progress and fighter for better housing. He received the honorary L.L.D. (doctorate) from Fordham University, the University of Notre Dame, and from the University of Michigan. He was president of the Pharmacists Association of Puerto Rico in 1938, and was elected president of the American Society for International Development, and the Foreign Service Association. He belongs to such clubs as the Bankers, the Hermitage, and Rho Chi fraternity in San Juan.

Moscoso would like to be remembered for his contribution to the improvement of life for the people of Latin America. His contributions to better housing, not only in Puerto Rico, but throughout Latin America shall be long remembered. I can still see the many blocks of public housing standing in San Juan all the way from the airport to the heart of the city. These are living memorials to the man who fought for better life of Spanish-speaking people . . . a man who is an evangelist for progress. Young Spanish-speaking children can take courage from Teodoro Moscoso who became chief (jefe) of the Alliance For Progress. They need to pick up where Moscoso had to leave off because of change in administration. Moscoso now lives back in his beloved Ponce, but he shared his life and talents with all of Latin America.

RICARDO MONTALBAN
ACTOR

One of the most versatile actors on television and in motion pictures today is Spanish-speaking, Mexican-born Ricardo Montalban. It has been said of Montalban that "even the most casual motion picture or television viewer must have the impression that Ricardo Montalban is conducting a one-man repertory theatre."

Actually, he could be on television more only if he had the lead in a TV series. But, he enjoys playing in different roles and different media, so he can be seen in Universal's "Sweet Charity" in which he co-stars with Shirley MacLaine and the movie "The SOB's" for Dino Di Laurentis.

On TV Ricardo has played a variety of characters, ranging from a superhuman in "Star Trek" to a kindly old White King in "Alice Through the Looking Glass." He played a priest in the "Longest 100 Miles," a Universal feature made for television. He played a killer in "Felony Squad," a South American dictator in "I Spy," then, an impoverished count in "Daniel Boone," plus the role of a foreign agent in a Bob Hope Chrysler program. Recently, Ricardo completed a pilot program for his own television series, "Deep Lab," produced by Universal Pictures and Ivan Tors.

Besides being an actor, Ricardo is a fine singer. Because of his quality singing voice, plus his distinguished performance, he won critical acclaim when he starred in the title role in "The King and I" at the Los Angeles Music Center.

Once cast only in Latin American lover-type roles, Ricardo has now been recognized for his multiple talents and bi-lingual ability. Producers now cast him in many different roles.

Ricardo Montalban was born in Mexico City, Mexico, on November 25, 1920, the son of the late Jeraro and Ricardo Montalban. He is the youngest of four children. His family moved to a ranch at Torreson in northern Mexico when financial problems plunged the father into bankruptcy. Ricardo's father was in the dry goods business. Ricardo learned to ride and swim with the great out-of-doors

57

as his playground. He received his early education at a Mexican parochial school, then followed his older brother to Los Angeles. There he continued his education at Fairfax High School.

While in high school Ricardo took part in numerous plays before graduation. He attracted the attention of studio talent scouts. Even though he was offered an MGM screen test after his high school graduation, he chose New York for his initial acting career. Ricardo felt New York would broaden his scope as an actor. At first he had a discouraging start. He found himself one of hundreds reading for the same part, as so often happens with young actors. Then his break came. He was cast with Tallulah Bankhead in "Her Cardboard Lover." From that point on, he became a highly successful stage actor and appeared in one theatre success following another.

But, Ricardo never forgot his native Mexico. In 1941 he returned to Mexico to make *nine* Spanish language films, all in a period of four years. His American movie success was made as an MGM contract actor in "Fiesta." Other pictures in which he appeared were "The Kissing Bandit," "Tortilla Flat," "Battleground," "Across the Wide Missouri," "On an Island with You," "Neptune's Daughter," "Sombrero," "Border Incident," and "Mystery Street."

He also appeared as a free-lance star. Ricardo was seen in "Sayonara," "Hemmingway's Adventures of a Young Man," "Saracen Blade," "Life in the Balance," and "Sol Madrid," to name but a few.

One of the highlights of Montalban's career was in the theatre in the national tour of Paul Gregory's "Don Juan in Hell." He won critical acclaim for his fine performance in this difficult play by George Bernard Shaw.

Ricardo is vitally interested in the improved status of Spanish-speaking persons. He wrote the author, "Please accept my respect and admiration for the work you are doing on behalf of Spanish-American people." Ricardo gives many hours to NOSOTROS, meaning *we*, a Hollywood based nonprofit organization working to improve the lot of Spanish-Americans. He is president of the organization. He says, "I have taken upon myself to answer each letter personally when my work permits." Replies include, he says, "Letters of complaint, requests for contributions and personal appearances, as well as praise and encouragement." He is extremely interested in the whole area of better human relations.

Ricardo is married to the former Georgiana Young, and they have two sons, Mark and Victory, and two daughters, Laura and Anita. They live in Hollywood Hills in what is described as a rambling ranch-type home. Ricardo still goes to Mexico occasionally to make Spanish-language films. He is a well-rounded athlete. He plays tennis, rides horseback, boxes occasionally, fences, and enjoys swimming in either California or Mexico. Ricardo stands five feet, 11 inches tall and weighs 170 pounds. He is distinguished by his brown hair and piercing brown eyes.

You may remember Ricardo Montalban in some of the following pictures in which he appeared: "Latin Lover," "Saracen Blade," "Green Shadows," "Right Cross," "The Black Pirate," "The Reluctant Saint," "My Man and I," "The Money Trap," "Let No Man Write My Epitaph," "Buenas Noches Ano Nuevo (Mexico)," "The Young Man," "Cheyenne Autumn," and "The Singing Nun."

Spanish-speaking persons can point with pride to the accomplishments of Ricardo Montalban who rose from the humble hills of Mexico to become one of the leading actors of television and movie screen in the United States, as well as in his beloved Mexico. Young Spanish-Americans have here a hero of the stage who is a hero also in real life.

MANUEL MARTINEZ SANTANA

TENNIS CHAMP

Assisted by Jennie Valasco

If you ask a lover of athletics, "Who is one of the world champions in tennis?" if he is knowledgeable, he will say MANUEL SANTANA. And Manuel Martinez Santana is Spanish, bringing honor to the Spanish-speaking people throughout the world.

Santana was born in the Madrid suburb of Chamanten, Spain, on May 10, 1938. His father was Bravlio Santana and his mother Mercedes Martinez. Manuel is one of four children. He had three brothers, Vraulio, Nicolas, and Victoriano.

Very early in life Manuel took a love for tennis. As early as ten years of age he quit school and became a ball boy at the Club Tenis de Velasquez in Madrid. His tennis playing began seriously at the age of thirteen. Unfortunately, Manuel's father, who was an electrician, died when Manuel was sixteen. But luck was on Manuel's shoulders and a family at the tennis club took him in and offered him an education. This lessened Manuel's mother's grief considerably, for he was well cared for. His host family, the Girons, were a very disciplined family. Therefore, Manuel had the benefit of

learning a demanding discipline. He was able to take tennis lessons in the mornings and work with a private tutor for his studies in the afternoon.

Very early in life Santana started winning tennis contests. In June, 1961, Manuel won the French clay court championship at the Roland Garros Stadium in Paris. This was no small feat, for the amateur he defeated was then considered the best player on clay courts. He beat Nicolas Pietrangeli. It was Santana who became the first Spaniard to win an international tennis championship. Then in Paris he won a second championship in 1964.

Santana then met the Americans in August, 1965 on the clay courts of Barcelona. The Santana team defeated the Americans for the Davis Cup competition with the trouncing defeat of four games to one. It was Frank Deford, sports writer

for the magazine, *Sports Illustrated,* who commented on the excellence of the match between Spain and the United States. He said that Santana was now the best clay court player in the world.

Deford pointed out that Santana possessed all the principle qualities of the well-rounded athlete — that is "courage, ability, competitiveness, and sportsmanship." It was the first time Spain had reached the Davis Cup challenge round when Santana competed in 1965. Manuel defeated Roy Emerson, which was so important, because Emerson had been undefeated in eight previous Davis Cup singles matches. And four hundred Spanish patriots had made the long trip to Australia to cheer Manuel on to victory. Upon the defeat of Emerson, the Spanish friends of Santana lifted him on their shoulders and carried him to his dressing room. Following his defeat by Santana, Emerson, who was then thirty, felt crushed and decided it was time for the younger players to compete. It appears that Emerson must have had a change of heart for he continued in tennis competition.

Santana learned early that life sometimes puts obstacles in the way of success. For unfortunately, Manuel had a fall during a tennis match in June, 1966. He injured his right ankle, which had been hurt formerly. But he was not discouraged. After a month's rest he returned to tennis competition. Soon he fell again and re-injured his ankle. But Manuel did fight his way to the semi finals, where he was eliminated by John Newcombe of Australia. Pain forced Manuel to have

surgery on his ankle in November of 1966. Fortunately, he soon recovered.

Manuel Santana is a versatile gentleman. Besides being a tennis player he has been a market representative for a tobacco company. He is five feet eight inches tall and weighs around 154 pounds. He has green eyes, and chestnut hair. He is said to have a charming face, despite a problem with protruding teeth. Santana is especially fond of music and collects records. His religion is Roman Catholic. For his hobbies he enjoys swimming, playing soccer, and seeing modern movies.

On September 9, 1962 Manuel Santana was married to Maria Fernandez Gonzalez Lopez. They have a daughter, Beatriz, and a son, Manuel, Jr.

Santana has received a number of honors. A special honor was the Gold Medal for Merit in Sports received from the government of Spain. In addition he was given the Gold Medal by the city of Madrid. Sportswriters like to describe Santana as an excellent tactician and a tennis player who plays with special precision. He remains amateur because he wants to compete in the Davis Cup contests. He feels he brings honor to his country by winning in the world competition.

Manuel Santana is an example of an athlete who would not give up despite his injuries and difficulties. Young Spanish-speaking athletes can take courage from this world tennis champion. Wouldn't you like to see Manuel whiz that tennis ball across the net to defeat his opponent? Perhaps you will.

DR. PEDRO C. SANCHEZ

UNIVERSITY PRESIDENT

Dr. Pedro C. Sanchez is a well-known educator from the Island of Guam. He comes from a family tradition of education, for his father was for many years the superintendent of the school system of the Island of Guam. Many persons say Pedro's father gave birth to the progressive school system on Guam and was instrumental in bringing higher education to this American territory in the Western Pacific.

Pedro was a very young man when the Japanese took over the Island during World War II. Many officers and G.I.s of the United States Armed Forces encouraged Pedro to go to college in the United States. For a time Pedro drove jeeps and personnel carriers for the Navy after the Island was liberated from the Japanese. In October of 1946 he arrived at St. Thomas College in St. Paul, Minnesota, to begin his undergraduate education under a generous scholarship provided by St. Thomas. He graduated with honors from St. Thomas in 1950 and returned to Guam where he taught at the high school. The people of Guam thought so much of Pedro that the political, business, and civic leaders put together a scholarship fund to get Pedro to the United States so he could pursue his graduate education. Pedro received his Master of Arts in Educational Administration from Columbia University in New York and then went to Stanford University where he received another scholarship. He was given the Ph.D. and became even more proficient in his speciality — school administration. Following his formal education Dr. Sanchez was extended a number of honors.

In 1961 he was a member of the United States delegation appearing before the United States Committee on Non-Self-Governing Territories. In 1963 he was a member of President Kennedy's White House Mission to the United States Trust Territory of the Pacific Islands. From 1965 to 1967 he was Chief of Human Resources and Urban Development for AID in Panama.

Dr. Sanchez has travelled extensively throughout Southeast Asia, the North

American Continent, and Central America. He is a native Guamanian. For a time, (1957-1961), Dr. Sanchez was president of the College of Guam and helped lay the plans which resulted in the organization of the University of Guam. It was in September, 1967, when the Island adopted the university structure with three undergraduate schools; a school of education, a school of arts and sciences, and a school of continuing education plus a graduate school. Each school now has its own dean. On August 12, 1968, Pedro Sanchez saw his College of Guam become the University of Guam. He did not know then that he would become the University's second president.

Along with Dr. Paul Carano, Dr. Sanchez wrote a book on *THE HISTORY OF GUAM.* Dr. Carano had worked with Pedro at Stanford University where each of them had worked in the School of Education. Both are now at the University of Guam.

With extensive experience in school administration, Dr. Sanchez, for a time, served as the Commissioner of Education in the Virgin Islands. He was then called on by the administration of President John F. Kennedy to serve as the Associate Director of the Peace Corps in the Philippines and later as Director of Peace Corps Training in Washington for Peace Corps volunteers going to the Far East. Jules Pagano, National Executive Director of the Adult Education Association and former Director of Training for the U. S. Peace Corps, says of Dr. Pedro Sanchez: "I think Pedro is an outstanding educator. He came in first every time after his Stanford Scholarship. He was responsible for training Peace Corps volunteers in the Philippines when I was the National Director of Training in Peace Corps under Sargent Shriver. Pedro had the largest Peace Corps project in education in the 1962-64 period. He was responsible for all volunteers going to that part of the country.

"We were proud that Pedro returned to become president of the University he helped plan.

"I recall that, in addition to his own children, he took under his wing a half dozen more children (mostly Guamanian) and clothed them, fed them, and educated them in the United States. At last he had the opportunity to return to his beloved Guam to serve his fellow countrymen and enlarge opportunities for youth and adults in higher education as president of the University of Guam."

Pedro is married to the former Florida Galeai, a native of American Samoa. They have seven children, Simon, Anthony and Lina born on Guam; Florida born in the Virgin Islands; Dolores born in the Philippines; Paul born in Panama; and Amanda born in Washington, D.C.

A visit with Dr. Joseph Leone, Director of Research and Public Service in Continuing Education at the University of Oklahoma, remembers Dr. Pedro Sanchez when Dr. Leone was a consultant evaluator in the Island of Guam. "I recall when Pedro was in charge of the regional office of the U.S. Office of Education in San Francisco in charge of adult education. He has a fine family. I think that the progress of education in Guam and the trust territory of 2100 islands will depend largely upon the leadership of Pedro Sanchez. He brings hundreds of teachers into the University of Guam for teacher training and will have a major impact."

In 1968-69 Dr. Sanchez was in charge of the Title I, Community Service and Continuing Education programs in the Division of Adult Education, United States Office of Education. Dr. Donald Deppe, now head of Title I programs says: "Dr. Sanchez came in and gave vigorous new leadership to the Community Service and Continuing Education Programs, a 9 and 1/2 million dollar program divided among fifty states. He is a warm and devout person who takes his faith and family very seriously."

Persons who have worked on the Island have felt the influence of Dr. Sanchez, even when for many years he was working in the continental United States. Dr. J. Robert Murray, Director of Instructional Resources Center for Indiana University of Pennsylvania served for two years as Director of the Multi-Media Services for the Guam Department of Education. He says of Dr. Sanchez, "To the people of Guam Dr. Sanchez is 'Mr. Education'. Because of his outstanding leadership in education throughout the world, Governor Carlos Camacho and the University's Board of Regents expended every effort to convince Dr. Sanchez to return to Guam from Washington, D.C., to be President of the University of Guam. The Sanchez family has had a major impact on improving life for the citizens of Guam."

Dr. Sanchez now heads the mult-million dollar university. For example, in 1968 the budget for the University of Guam was $1,608,177 while today the budget reported for 1969 was $3,392,870, a marked increase. Since his appointment, he has succeeded in obtaining a budget of $6.9 million — a 48% increase to the previous years. The enrollment is now over 2,500 students. New buildings include a new science building, health science building, a student center, and three dormitory buildings. Guam now has the 200th Educational Television station for spreading knowledge, with a University of the Air.

Pedro Sanchez is an example of a young man who dedicated himself to improving mankind through education. He can make a major contribution to education through his leadership as President of the University of Guam.

JOE KAPP

MEXICAN-AMERICAN FOOTBALL CHAMP

"He's got what it takes to be a winning quarterback," says Jim Finks, the Viking professional football general manager who brought Joe Kapp from Canada. Joe had played in Canada for eight years but got national recognition when he came to the United States to play for the Vikings.

Joe Kapp was born in rural New Mexico in 1938. He grew up in Salinas and Newhall, California. His mother came from Mexico, and his father was from Germany. We are told his mother made a living as a waitress, supporting five children. As a boy, Joe was extremely fond of basketball. Why? "Because," Joe said, "you can play it alone. But, I was always a quarterback in my mind." So, football was his goal. He always wanted to be a quarterback. Joe found that he liked to command. He liked to be in control, and his wife says it's true in every situation.

Following high school, Joe decided to go to the University of California. He played basketball, but he also enjoyed playing football. He played basketball for Pete Newell, and football for Pete Elliott. He also learned to box and always had a desire to fight in Madison Square Garden.

Joe feels there is a "tingle in boxing" and adds, "I've always been a boxing fan." But the nearest Joe came to boxing at "The Garden" was a boxing match on the basketball court when his California team played Temple. Says Joe, "The coach put me into the game, and I got into a fight with Van Patton." When Joe punched Van Patton in the knee, the referee kicked both players out of the game. But, Joe thought it a good deal. Van Patton had scored 28, and Joe recalls he himself made only 2.

Kapp was a physical education major and a scholarship football player at Berkeley. He had a job while in school but says it didn't take much of his time. It appears Joe became a bit of a philosopher while at Berkeley. Joe says, "When I went there, I didn't know what a Jew was; some kind of Philistine, I thought. And to me there was no black problem. So I got to Berkeley, and I found out."

67

Joe Kapp seems to make friends easily. He even has friends among the defensive teams. Joe's idea is that the "team is more important than the individual." That's a mighty important thing to remember when men are blocking for a quarterback like Joe. He likes to think of himself like Zorba the Greek. Joe feels that he has to be himself and that he has to be honest with himself and with others. Two important pointers this football hero makes: "One man is not more important than another," and "you have to work within your limits."

One *New York Times* reporter describes Joe as "crude but successful." Joe doesn't like this description, and his green eyes can flash with anger. He wants to know if the writer means "not graceful" when he says "crude"? His sharp comeback is "Well, they pay a quarterback to win, not on how pretty he looks." Most of us would agree that is a good comeback.

Lonnie Warwick of the Vikings thinks of Joe Kapp as a winner. Lonnie said of Joe, "But you can tell he's a winner. And there's no quarterback as tough. When they punish him, he just gets up and laughs." And Alex Karras, Detroit's vocal defensive lineman says of Joe, "As a quarterback he's got no class, but he gets the job done."

Leonard Shecter, the *Look* magazine sports editor knew Joe as "the joyously rough and tough quarterback of the Minnesota Vikings." (Actually, Joe Kapp is now with the Boston Patriots) It was in the Viking game against the Los Angeles Rams that Kapp got to the hearts and minds of the team. The story is told that Joe bent over his center, glared at the Rams' line, and yelled loudly, clearly, and distinctly, "youxxxxRams!"

Joe Kapp has leadership ability, what Ed Sharockman calls "charisma," the quality of leading his teammates. But Joe has more than that. One writer says "He has the nerve of a pickpocket, the confidence of a street brawler, and each time he is tested, he adds even more glitter to that charisma (leadership)."

Joe is a man of action. He is impatient with talk. He believes that cussing out the linemen is the coaches' dirty job, not his. He tries to give encouragement. Joe says, "I try to pick them up rather than take them down." Joe's ability to take it as well as dish it out is a quality other football players admire. And a quarterback takes a lot of bumps in a football game. Says Mich Tingelhoff, a Viking center, "I've seen Joe get hurt, really dumped, and he comes back with fire in his eyes and a smile on his face. You play better for a guy like that." This is the kind of support a man needs from fellow football players.

And Joe is not one to blame his blockers. Bud Grant, head coach of the Vikings, says he likes the way Joe carries himself on the field. Grant commended Joe's ability to take it, "It's one thing to be tough, and another to react the way Joe does. He'll stand back there and get absolutely hammered, and you'll never see him get up and point a finger at his blockers."

Joe compares the football game to the bullfights. He says it's like the lions and ancient Christians. Joe has known some real hardships. For example, he once got a broken beer bottle across the face from a Canadian teammate who was mentally deranged. That same teammate later shot a priest. A long scar reminds Joe of the incident which required 110 stitches. Some feel the scar adds to a feeling that Joe is one of the toughest you will come across in football. And there is little doubt that he is.

Joe knows winning, but he also knows losing, too. In his eight years in Canada he played for Calgary and for Vancouver. His coaches say he learned the game well. Grant says, "He's done it all. He's had the winning and the losing; he's played when he was hurt, and he's had the good days and the bad." And Joe has had his share of injuries. In a game with Baltimore, Joe broke his left wrist. But that did not put him out. He played with a cast and never missed a minute of the game. The Colts won that game, but he met them the next year and threw seven touchdown passes, winning the game for the Vikings, 52-14. In Spanish he would say, "La venganza es dulce!" — the vengence is sweet!

Joe enjoys his 1939 La Salle antique car which we are told he keeps spotless. His wife Marcia has been a great help to Joe. They have a son, J.J. Bumper, who wears large round glasses and is said to be mighty bright. Joe enjoys nothing more than romping with his seven year old son, Joseph John.

Joe knows football is a rough and rugged game, but it is in his blood. "You got to be crazy to play this game . . . It makes you crazy," says Joe Kapp. But he seems to enjoy the football fight, for he always comes back for more! The sports world can be proud of Joe Kapp who describes himself humorously as "Half-Mexican — Half-Gringo."

(The author is indebted to Leonard Schecter, Look Sports Editor, for selected biographical material.)

JIM PLUNKETT
FOOTBALL CHAMPION

"Thus far, I believe Jim Plunkett is the best college quarterback I've ever seen," said Bud Wilkinson, TV football analyst and championship coach of University of Oklahoma. "Plunkett is the best pro quarterback prospect I've ever seen," commented Tommy Prothro, University of California at Los Angeles (UCLA) head coach.

Of Mexican descent, Jim Plunkett has made a national reputation in football. Born in San Jose, California, on December 5, 1947, Jim has withstood tremendous pressures both on the football field and in life. We might wonder if we could have overcome the obstacles? Jim's father was afflicted with progressive blindness and died in the spring of 1969. His mother, who is totally blind, met her husband at a school for the blind in New Mexico. His father worked in restaurants, spent years as a news vender, and was well-known as a worker in the San Jose Post Office before he died. From his dad Jim learned the meaning of hard work as a boy. He worked long hours as a grocery clerk while he was in high school. Also, Jim was a gas station attendant and worked as a paper boy to help his family earn a living.

Jim Plunkett first played football in the 5th grade at Mayfair Elementary School on San Jose's east side. (He sprained his ankle playing guard in the 6th grade). In 7th grade a bone disease limited his football but he played some baseball. He started playing quarterback when he was in the 8th grade. It was then he found out his special skill. He says, "I found out I could throw." And he has been throwing passes ever since. His 8th grade junior high team won the county championship.

Jim loved all sports. He wrestled, played basketball, ran in track meets, and played baseball, in addition to his football activity. He was a top rebounder and scorer in basketball. In track he specialized in triple jump and high jump. He played pitcher and outfielder for the baseball team.

At Overfeldt High School, in his first year, he was too big for the B team but just too young for the varsity. So he played quarterback for the junior varsity. Jim had a knee injury when a sophomore, but for protection he taped his knees tightly each game. For his junior year he played for James Lick High School standing 6-3 and weighing 215 pounds. He led James Lick's squad to an 8-1 record winning the Mt. Hamilton Athletic League. Jim was named All-League proving himself one of Northern California's top high school passers. He was quiet, unassuming, and anything but brash or boastful. He still is!

His senior year at James Lick he sparked the team to a 9-0 record. Again named to the All-League team, Jim said in his senior year he "ran more and threw better." Named to the North Shrine All-Star Team, he played defensive halfback proving how versatile he is. But, Jim had his eyes focused on Stanford University.

Jim wanted to stay close to his parents, partly because of their blindness. Of Stanford Jim says, "I was interested in the football potential at Stanford, and of course, the academic reputation of the University is well-known." But Jim had hard luck at the outset at Stanford. In his early days it was discovered he had a thyroid tumor, deep in the left side of his neck. Requiring surgery, September, 1966, found Jim recovering in a hospital. He was out of the early games but started at quarterback in the last three games. He said "I played badly" but refused to be discouraged and worked doubly hard in

spring practice in 1967. Coach John Ralston had Gene Washington at quarterback, plus two other excellent quarterbacks. "I really had a poor spring," says Plunkett, "and I could tell I had a long way to go before being a capable varsity player." All summer he threw that football and built back his health. "I thought I could play in the fall," said Jim, "but the quarterback position was really jammed up with a lot of people. It was hard for me to break into the lineup. When I didn't make the trip for the opening game against Oregon State, I thought maybe I would still have a chance when the team came home. But Marquess started at quarterback against Kansas, and later Chuck Williams took over. However, both coaches advised Jim not to throw away a whole year of eligibility late in the season. He agreed and laid out.

Then, Jim had his opportunity! In 1968 he made 14 touchdowns, and completed 142 passes out of 268 attempted. In '69 he completed 197 passes of 336 for 2,673 yards, making 20 touchdowns. In 1970 Jim broke many records! He ended his career with 7,887 yards. Never before in the 101 year history of college football has any player gone over 7,000 yards. And he walked away with the following honors the greatest of which is the Heisman Trophy, *football's highest award;* Maxwell Trophy, United Press International Player of the Year; Sporting News Player of the Year; Walter Camp All-American Committee Player of the Year; American College Football Coaches Association Offensive Player of the Year; UPI Back of the Year; Voit Memorial

Trophy Winner; First Team All-American (UPI, Sporting News, Football Writers' Ass'n/*Look* Magazine, American College Football Coaches Association/Kodak, Walter Camp, Time, NEA, Central Press captains); Second Team All-American (AP); 1st Team All-Coast (AP, UPI); 1st Team All Pacific-8 Conference. And Jim holds the NCAA Career Passing record of 7,544 yards, formerly held by Steve Ramsey, North Texas State 1967-69.

Jim broke the record for the longest touchdown pass play with 96 yards, Plunkett to Randy Vataha, vs. Washington State in 1970. The former record was 93 yards. Jim is known as the "record breaker."

In the Pacific-8 Career:
Net Yards Passing — 7,544 (former record 4,501, Craig Morton, 1962-64)

Yards Total Offense — 7,887 (former record 5,358, Gary Beban, UCLA, 1965-67)

Pass Completions — 530 (former record 355, Graig Morton, 1962-64)

Touchdown passes — 52 (former record 37, Bob Berry, Oregon, 1962-64)

Plunkett already holds every Pacific-8 Conference season and career record in total offense, passing and TD passes.

But, Jim is also a student! He wants to make a good scholastic record. Plunkett's ambitions do not end on the football field. He is a "B" student in political science and comments, "the fact that Stanford is so good educationally is the main reason I came back the extra year." It should be remembered Jim did not play his sophomore season and could have made himself eligible for the professional draft a year earlier than normal, since his class graduated in June 1969. Even if he plays pro-football, Jim plans to attend Stanford either in the Law School or the Business School when he is not on the gridiron.

"Plunkett is big, strong, and smart; he'll probably be the first guy selected in the pro-draft" says Gil Brandt, (he was) the personnel director of the Dallas Cowboys who is always on the lookout for talent. And Jim's all around ability is varified by John McKay, University of Southern California head coach who said "Plunkett is the strongest college quarterback I've ever seen. He's not just a dropback passer. He can do a lot of other things well. He can half-roll, scramble, run when he's in trouble and get rid of the ball with guys hanging on."

Plunkett is unquestionably one of America's greatest quarterbacks ever to play college football. He won the Rose Bowl for Stanford in 1970, and great things lie ahead. Collegiate history will undoubtedly know him as *"JIM PLUNKETT — FOOTBALL CHAMPION!"*

Now Jim Plunkett begins a new era. He has turned professional. He must now meet the challenge of competition with the world's greatest football giants. If he lives up to his past record and reputation, football fans have some exciting gridiron action in store for them. Keep an eye on Jim Plunkett!

VINCENTE T. XIMENES
PUBLIC SERVANT

Born in Floresville, Texas, on December 5, 1919, Vincente T. Ximenes was the fifth child of seven children born to the Mexican-American family of Mr. and Mrs. Jose F. Ximenes. Vincente dreamed of having an opportunity to go to school and earn a degree. He entered the Floresville High School in Texas and made a good record. He enjoyed sports but studied hard and had his eye on a college education. He was particularly interested in social problems and determined to do something significant for the Spanish-speaking people. He finished high school and was accepted at the University of New Mexico and decided to work toward a degree in economics. He was awarded the Bachelor of Arts degree in 1951 from the University of New Mexico and went on for graduate work. He attended the University of Texas and obtained the Master of Arts degree in Economics. All the time he had his eye on government service.

Early in his career he served as an elementary school teacher in a little town of Picosa, Texas, during 1940 and 1941. For a period of ten years he served as a Research Economist for the University of New Mexico from 1951 to 1961. He learned of the inequalities of opportunity for minority groups, and he decided to see if he could not help the plight of the Mexican-American. He felt that he could make a major contribution in the government service, and determined to become a public servant. Then an unusual opportunity was offered him. His Spanish background held him in good stead, and he was offered a position with the Agency for International Development with an opportunity to go to Ecuador. The position was Program Officer and Economist for the AID in Quito, Ecuador. He served in this position in the high mountains of Ecuador for three years from 1961 through 1964. Then Vincente T. Ximenes took on a major political assignment. He was made the director of the VIVA Johnson-Humphrey Campaign for the United States and traveled widely

75

in behalf of the Democratic party. From September, 1964, through December of that year he assembled Spanish-speaking persons into support for President Lyndon Johnson and Vice-President Hubert Humphrey. He gained many friends among the Mexican-Americans throughout the Southwest and became known as one of the leaders in the Democratic party. Then came the opportunity for service in Washington, D.C. President Johnson was returned to office, and Vincente Ximenes was offered the post of Assistant to the Inspector General in the Office of Economic Opportunity. In his position Vincente was able to influence some of the direction of the O.E.O. to help improve the status and economic conditions of Spanish-speaking people. Both Mexican-Americans and the American Indians were given some major grants to help alleviate the poverty conditions in the Southwest. Then the Agency for International Development again called on Vincente Ximenes for help. They asked him if he would serve as the Deputy Director of the AID Mission to Panama. He served in this position from 1966 through 1967. As an outgrowth of his fine record, he was called on by the President to take a new assignment as the Chairman of the Cabinet Committee on Mexican-American Affairs in Washington, D.C. He served in this position from 1967 through 1969. He was influencial in civil rights legislation and in fair employment practice cases.

Because of his experience and dedication to the principles of fair employment in 1967, he was asked if he would serve as a member of the President's Commission on Equal Employment Opportunity. He accepted that position and has served in Washington as a member of the Commission for four years. He handles cases of alleged discrimination for any minority persons, not just Mexican-Americans.

Vincente T. Ximenes has had a number of honors and awards. He was the recipient of the United Nations Human Rights Award, and was given the G.I. Forum National Leadership Award for his work with the Spanish-speaking G.I.'s. He is a board member of Reading is Fundamental National Advisory Board and received a fellowship to the Race-Relations Institute at Fisk University. He is a member of a number of professional honorary scholastic fraternities including Phi Kappa Phi and Phi Delta Kappa, the national fraternity for excellent speakers.

Most Spanish-speaking adults have heard of the G.I. Forum which has assisted in legislation for civil rights. Perhaps Vincente Ximenes is most proud of being the founder of the American G.I. Forum of New Mexico and served for two years as the national chairman. He served honorably as an Air Force Major from 1941 through 1947 and was the recipient of the Distinguished Flying Cross.

Here is a man who moved all the way from being a chief clerk in the Civilian Conservation Corps Camp in Floresville and Segiun, Texas, in 1939 to becoming a member of the President's Equal Employment Opportunity Commission in Washington, D.C. He feels that being a public servant is a high honor, and he has served with distinction.

In 1943 Vincente married the former Maria Castillo of San Antonio, Texas. They have four children — Steve, Ricardo, Olivia, and Ana Maria. Vincente T. Ximenes is never happier than when at home surrounded by his wife and children.

He is the author of several research publications dealing with economics and a number of government reports dealing with the Agency for International Development experience. He would like to see more opportunities extended to Spanish-speaking young people, and he is working hard toward that end. He hopes more young people will enter government service and become public servants.

DR. AURORA P. GUARDIOLA

CUBAN EXILE PROFESSOR

In the tropical Island of Cuba in Havana City, Aurora P. Guardiola was born the second daughter of a total of four girls. Her father worked as a businessman for 38 years in order to enjoy his retirement, but he finally lost everything when he came to the United States for political reasons.

Raised in a middleclass home, Aurora's parents gave their children a good education and a very pleasant childhood and adolescence. Aurora recalls, "We were a very big family because my parents raised my mother's nine brothers and sisters when her mother died, and over there I enjoyed all my life in a happy environment. The things that most interest me are reading, painting, writing poems and knitting, which my grandmother taught me. Sewing, I learned from my mother. I learned how to read when I was four years old in a private school, and since that time my teaching vocation began, and in my house I repeated to empty chairs all the lessons I received. My parents used to tell me that I explained the lessons so well that their friends came to see my teaching. I studied in a private Catholic School, both elementary and high school. I remember especially one of my teachers, a nun, Madre Maria'. I do not forget that I always would speak too much and her wise advice was, 'If you are going to say something, think three times before saying it and then . . . . do not say it'. I recognize that I do not practice her advice as much as I should. Sometimes this nun prepared a group of us for a recital, songs and popular music we performed, and took us to a hospital where the lepers lived. How deeply I thanked God for the health I had. I remember the good example they gave me with their resigned illness and how happy they became with what we did for them!"

I asked Dr. Guardiola, "Why did you happen to enter teaching?" "When I started in school I followed the example of all my teachers. I even dressed like them. My first teacher, Miss Carmela was a great teacher. Because I liked her as a

79

teacher, I wanted to follow in her footsteps. At that time I was determined to enter her career. I have only been sorry once, that was when I resigned as a teacher, because I was asked to impose the Communist doctrine. I refused to do it."

A major influence on Dr. Guardiola was the then Secretary of Education, Dr. Hernández. She tells, "When I was studying in the Havana State Teachers College I was very lucky in having, in my junior year, Dr. Alicia Hernández as a mathematics professor. She proved to be an intellectual woman, a writer, and deeply involved in politics. She was Secretary of Education at that time. She was the one who influenced me more in my future when I saw her dedication to the students and to scholarship. I hate math, but in her classes I got A's. But more than anything I liked her behavior and justice as a professor. She inspired me very much. Sometimes when I had to make important decisions, her example guided me."

When Aurora graduated from Havana State Teachers College, she began her studies in Havana University for a Doctorate in Education. Says Dr. Guardiola, "I got my teaching position in elementary school by a contest system. This means that in order to get the job, one has to be number one in an examination among all the teachers that have applied for that job. After several years teaching and working in the community I was recognized with a reward and a diploma titled: 'The Best Teacher of the Year'."

Independence Day in Cuba was on May the twentieth and on that day Aurora went to an official ceremony with her students. Says Aurora of that day, "And over there my life changed forever because I met my husband, Antonio. Antonio is also a teacher. His field was math and English. Now he teaches Spanish in the University. Two years later we married and since that time all my life changed and I started the happy stage of being a married woman. We had, as everybody does, both happy and difficult times. I was dedicated completely to my profession, and still am. However, my role as a woman took first place."

Dr. Guardiola tells of becoming an administrator. She recalls, "I realized that I wanted to work in the capital city of Havana and I became the principal of one elementary school, supervising seventeen teachers. But I was eager to work with teenagers and later on my dreams came true when I went to another contest and I got a teaching position in Havana City. I taught again, but this time in a high school, Enrique José Varona High School, named after one of our philosophers and a great teacher.

Dr. Guardiola remembers vividly her experiences before she and her husband went into exile. She relates, "At that time I was very happy and very much involved in student social activities. Then the Communist regime took over the country, and there was lack of freedom and I resigned because I thought that my mission as an educator could not be fulfilled. The hardest decision for me was when I had to leave my country for political reasons. I had visited this country before as a tourist in the United States, and it is different. I am a Catholic and since the first moment I felt repulsion for the Communist doctrine they wanted to impose on me. Finally my husband and I went into exile. That hurt me forever! First, we went to Mexico City in 1963 and from there we came to the United States in 1964. I did not want to teach again because I suffered too much when I resigned as a teacher, and I cried what we call ' lágrimas de sangre ' (blood tears). Actually, I was planning to work in another job."

Dr. Guardiola tells how they happened to go into teaching in the United States. She says "We were living in Miami, which is called the New Havana, when my husband read an advertisement asking for university graduates for teaching Spanish in Pennsylvania. We went to an institute at Kutztown State College in order to know the American society and school laws and the educational system in this country, and methods of teaching the foreign languages. Then my husband was hired to teach at Indiana State College in Pennsylvania. We arrived in Indiana, Pennsylvania, September 1st, without money and I had no job. The next day Laura Lamar High School and Homer City Elementary School hired me as a Spanish teacher. Then the big problem started. I did not speak English at that time and I said to myself, "I will learn it speaking to the people and reading it," and decided not to be isolated because of the language barrier. No wonder I said yes to everything they were asking me in the

interview with the superintendent and the principal of the school! Later I realized that I made too many mistakes. Fortunately, four months later I was hired for teaching in Indiana State College, too. That college is now Indiana University of Pennsylvania where I am still very happy to work. I teach Spanish to both college students and adults. I am teaching a group of adults in a class called 'Spanish for Travelers and Businessmen!'."

Dr. Guardiola found adjustments to living in midwestern United States a challenge. Adapting rapidly she relates, "We started enjoying our new life in the United States. Besides the language problem, the worst for me was the adaptation to life as an American woman, I mean to be a professor and at the same time to cook, to clean, to iron and all the things as a housewife. This was the big problem because in Cuba I always had a servant. I tried hard and now I can do it like any other American woman, but it caused me a lot of troubles."

The Guardiolas are cosmopolitan citizens and have traveled widely. Regarding travel she says, "We both like to travel and we have visited different states in the east and mid-west from New York to Key West, Florida and countries like Canada, Mexico, Spain and all over Cuba from east to west."

Dr. Guardiola sees the United States as a land of opportunity. Her feelings are: "I believe that the United States is the best place to live if one must leave his home country, because there are so many opportunities for everybody. But the things that have impressed me most are

81

how humanitarian people are, the freedom that one feels in all ways and the capacity of work of everybody. Americans are really good workers in all aspects! And what was hard for me to understand when I came was the concept of saving time, saving money, and the rush. For me, to talk with friends for hours, to watch the sky silently, to listen to music on the patio without hurry is more important than anything."

As we visited about her exile and about her experiences, Dr. Guardiola became philosophical. She says, "I would like to stress that to be a Spanish-speaking person, if one is a teacher, has both advantages and disadvantages. One can teach the language and compare cultures and understand the youth better. The disadvantage is that some people here think that all that they do, eat, feel, etc., is the best. But when they meet somebody born in a different country, they realize the differences and they accept them openly. I have been living in this country for eight years. I became an American citizen, and I thank God every morning for being in the United States, this great and free country. I am very, very happy here, even if you can hear me singing a Cuban music song: 'Mi Cuba te extrano͂, y no soy feliz', meaning "My Cuba, I miss you, that is why I cannot be happy."

LEE TREVINO
GOLF'S UNDISPUTED STAR

"I haven't even finished the eighth grade, and I can hardly count to 72, but then, I don't very often have to," laughed Lee Trevino, the only man in history ever to sweep the United States, British and Canadian golf championships in a row. "People don't care whether I can spell birdies, bogies, or par. They just want to see how I do it," smiled Trevino during a rainy day interview at the Ligonier, Pennsylvania Holiday Inn.

Surrounded by interested fans who love to hear his wisecracks, Trevino admitted he enjoys playing to his public. "Keep the public happy," volunteered Lee as he sat and grinned at my two friends and me. "I have to be sharp," says Lee, "I have to be faster than Bob Hope, and I might insult folks once in a while, but it brings humor. It's easy to play golf. The hardest thing is to deal with the public." And Trevino plays not only to win, but to bring fun to the game of golf.

One question, and Lee was off. "Do you feel it an advantage or handicap to be a Mexican-American?" "It's been no great handicap," came back Lee. "The way I feel, there is all the opportunity in the world if you want to work, and try and do for your country. I agree with Presi-

dent John F. Kennedy, 'Don't ask what your country can do for you, ask what you can do for your country.' We have a country which can provide for everyone, that's one thing about living in a country like America. I'm a perfect example."

Lee wanted to talk about his favorite charity, the El Paso Boy's Club. "I do a lot for charity," said Lee, "I don't want to work just for one group. We're trying to get people together. In my youth centers we work for all. I'm a Mexican born in America, and I get stacks of mail asking me, "Are you a Chicano?" I answer I'm a Mexican-American. Our youth centers are for *all* youth, Mexican, Negro, Italian, or Jewish.

Lee has become famous for his wise cracking. Since winning that first U.S. Open triumph, Lee has won more than $700,000. He finished among the top ten in 79 tournaments, collecting more than any other golfer on the tour in 1970. He quipped to one sports writer, "You can call me a Spaniard now, because who ever heard of a rich Mexican?" He loves to play golf, and told me that for fourteen weeks in a row he played daily, 97 rounds in 97 days.

Lee loves to talk about his children. He's 31 and has three youngsters, Ricky Lee, Leslie, and Tony Lee. He admits he only gets home about four times a year now, because he is so busy playing golf. "Mostly, my wife has to raise the kids," volunteered Lee. When I asked him "What are your hopes for your children?" his eyes sparkled.

"I want my kids to have the things I didn't have. I like to spoil them. When they see something and like it, I buy it for them. They'll realize someday we had hard times." Lee said he especially wants his children to get a chance to have a good education. He wants them to go to college.

Trevino wanted to talk about physical fitness. He is proud to be a member of the President's Conference on Physical Fitness, and Sports, and offered the following advice when asked 'Do you have any advice for men in the U.S.?'

"Regardless what business you are in, young or old, don't eat past six p.m. The trouble with men today is that 60% of them are overweight. They come home, eat, drink, watch TV, fall asleep, and end up with heart attacks. Food turns to fat when you're sleeping. Eat a big breakfast, a light dinner, and don't eat past 6 in the evening." He was adamant on this point.

Lee next talked about education. "Kids can't do without it," he said. "I work a lot with dropouts, and I ask the 16 year olds, 'What do you want to do with your life?' 90% of kids become dropouts because they get behind in their studies. They get bored. They're afraid, and they are ashamed to ask for help. Nothing makes a kid happier than to make straight A's. One of our problems is hiring good teachers. They have to be able to get ideas over to kids, and the importance of giving special help." He spoke of his daughter who he said did not go to preschool but has learned her ABC's, counts to 10,000, can write her name, and "learns from all her friends." But he thinks she will be bored in the first grade. "It's the same problem with high school, too many kids are bored," Lee thinks. Boredom, he feels, is the cause for lots of youth taking dope. His advice to teachers, "We need to communicate to the kids. We need to help the child move up," and Lee thinks tutoring is an answer. "I ask students, 'do you have a trade?' There is no better example than me. I didn't even finish 8th grade. I ask them, 'What the hell do you want to be?' Today you can't even pump gas at a filling station without a high school education. I'm just the luckiest guy in the world." Then he added, "It's easy to hit a golf ball." He next wanted to talk about his two-year-old.

84

"My boy is going to be the greatest golfer in the world. He's two years old and putts on the green. He watches me and imitates. I never have to tell him how to hold a club. He keeps his head down, and has a fine golf grip each time. He's a natural." Lee thinks children learn best by imitation.

Lee is very much an extrovert. He has a great sense of obligation to the public. He says, "I was born to serve people. I'd like to serve the public. And I want to help people." He is very proud of his work for charities such as cancer, TB, and the Boys Clubs.

"Are there persons or a person who most helped you when things were hard going?" I asked.

"Yes, Jesse and Don Whittington, who first put me on the professional golf tour, are my partners now. Jesse, you remember, used to be with the Green Bay Packers. We're in business together building apartments now, and involved in other investments."

Trevino is described as the duffer's delight. "I've got a lot of people rooting for me," Lee told one reporter, "because there's more poor people than rich people. You look at my galleries. You'll see tatoos (Lee has one on his left arm), plain dresses. I represent the guy who goes to the driving range, the municipal player, the truck driver, the union man, the guy who grinds it out. To them I am someone who worked hard, kept at it and made it. Sure, I go out of my way to talk to them. They're my people."[1]

[1]Time Magazine, July 19, 1971. p. 48.

"I hope to play golf until I die," Trevino said laughingly. "Practice makes perfect, is still true, and I just try two times as hard. You have to try to outdo, that's all. Know your product, and pitch twice as hard, that's what I believe." Then he concluded, "My one hope is to die on the 18th hole with a three footer!"